Resources from MOPS

Books

Beyond Macaroni and Cheese
The Birthday Book
Children Change a Marriage
A Cure for the Growly Bugs and Other Tips for Moms
Getting Out of Your Kids' Faces and into Their Hearts
In the Wee Hours
Loving and Letting Go
Make Room for Daddy
Meditations for Mothers
Mom to Mom
A Mother's Footprints of Faith
Ready for Kindergarten
Real Moms
What Every Child Needs
What Every Mom Needs

Little Books for Busy Moms Series

Boredom Busters
Great Books to Read and Fun Things to Do with Them
If You Ever Needed Friends, It's Now
Juggling Tasks, Tots, and Time
Kids' Stuff and What to Do with It
Planes, Trains, and Automobiles . . . with Kids!
Time Out for Mom . . . Ahhh Moments

Books with Drs. Henry Cloud and John Townsend

Raising Great Kids
Raising Great Kids for Parents of Preschoolers Workbook
Raising Great Kids for Parents of Teenagers Workbook
Raising Great Kids for Parents of School-Age Children Workbook

Gift Books

God's Words of Life from the Mom's Devotional Bible
Mommy, I Love You Just Because

Kids Books

Little Jesus, Little Me
My Busy, Busy Day
See the Country, See the City
Mommy, May I Hug the Fishes?
Mad Maddie Maxwell
Zachary's Zoo
Morning, Mr. Ted
Boxes, Boxes Everywhere
Snug as a Bug?

Bible

Mom's Devotional Bible

Audio Pages®

Raising Great Kids

Curriculum

Raising Great Kids for Parents of Preschoolers ZondervanGroupware™
(with Drs. Henry Cloud and John Townsend)

MOTHERS OF
MOPS.
PRESCHOOLERS

...because mothering matters

Exploding the Myths
of MOTHERHOOD

real MOMS

Elisa Morgan
Carol Kuykendall

ZONDERVAN™

GRAND RAPIDS, MICHIGAN 49530 USA

We want to hear from you. Please send your comments about this book to us in care of the address below. Thank you.

GRAND RAPIDS, MICHIGAN 49530 USA

WWW.ZONDERVAN.COM

ZONDERVAN™

Real Moms
Copyright © 2002 by MOPS International, Inc.

Requests for information should be addressed to:
Zondervan, *Grand Rapids, Michigan 49530*

Library of Congress Cataloging-in-Publication Data

Morgan, Elisa, 1955-
 Real moms : exploding the myths of motherhood / Elisa Morgan and
 Carol Kuykendall.
  p. cm.
 Includes bibliographical references.
 ISBN 0-310-24703-9
 1. Mothers—Religious life. 2. Motherhood—Religious aspects—Christianity.
3. Motherhood in popular culture—United States. I. Kuykendall, Carol, 1945– .
II. Title.
BV4529.18.M665 2002
248.8'431—dc21

                   2002008240

Published in association with the literary agency of Alive Communications, Inc., 7680 Goddard Street, Suite 200, Colorado Springs, CO 80920.

Interior design by Todd Sprague

Printed in the United States of America

04 05 06 /❖ DC/ 10 9 8 7 6 5 4

For every mom
who wants to be real

Contents

Acknowledgments 9

Real Moms 11

Introduction: The Myths of Motherhood 13

Part 1: Myths about Me

Chapter 1. Real Me Mom

Real Moms Know and Accept Who They Are 23

Chapter 2. Perma-Guilt Mom

Real Moms Feel Guilty 36

Chapter 3. Monster Mom

Real Moms Get Angry 47

Chapter 4. Please Everyone Mom

Real Moms Can't Fix Everyone and Everything 58

Chapter 5. Lookin' Good Enough Mom

Real Moms Struggle with Their Looks 69

Chapter 6. Viagra Mom

Real Moms Aren't Always in the Mood for Sex 81

Part 2: Myths about Mothering

Chapter 7. Doin' My Best Mom

Real Moms Aren't Perfect and Don't Have Perfect Children 95

Chapter 8. Mommy Wars Mom

Real Moms Like Their Way Best 104

Chapter 9. S.O.S. Mom

Real Moms Need Help 114

Chapter 10. Busy Mom
Real Moms Have Too Much to Do   125

Chapter 11. Worry-Some Mom
Real Moms Worry about Their Kids   136

Chapter 12. Control Freak Mom
Real Moms Can't Control How Their Kids Turn Out   148

Part 3: Myths about More Than Mothering

Chapter 13. Truth is Our Friend Mom
Real Moms Know the Truth Is Scary and Can Hurt   161

Chapter 14. Soul Mom
Real Moms Are More Than Moms   169

Chapter 15. Forever Mom
Real Moms Know Mothering Gets Different, Not Easier   178

Conclusion: Get Real!   187

Notes   189

Acknowledgments

Let's be real!

That's what this book is all about—the myths that moms face and the truth that sets us free to be real!

The words on these pages are the result of a team effort. First, we gratefully acknowledge the honesty of moms all around the country who gave us their reflections about real moms. They completed the sentence "Real moms . . ." and their definitions are sprinkled throughout the pages of this book.

The book also grows out of our experiences of working with moms through MOPS International, an organization founded in 1973 to nurture moms of young children. These experiences are filtered through our grid of mothering our own children (a combined total of five children over many years!) and our personal passion to grow more real as we continue to grow up.

Other real people who helped at MOPS International include Gail Burns, our faithful word-checker, who typed and retyped our drafts and checked and rechecked our sources; our readers, including Carla Barnhill, Michele Hall, Beth Jusino, Mary Beth Lagerborg, Karen Parks, Brenda Quinn, and Shelly Radic; our loyal executive assistant, Cyndi Bixler; Rick Christian and Chip MacGregor, our advocates at Alive Communications; and our editor Sandy Vander Zicht at Zondervan.

Each chapter in this book deals with a different myth and reality. Though we hope you read it cover to cover, we know that real moms are real busy. Some moms easily get real bored. You will know what encouragement you need most at the moment, and by looking at the chapter titles, you can zoom directly to that spot in the book. Different myths and realities may apply to you at different levels, depending upon your current challenge. Each chapter contains a How To sidebar of application, a Real Mom Story, some Reality Checks or questions for reflection or discussion, and some suggestions for further reading.

We invite you to join us on a personal journey through these pages, with our prayer that these real words will help you shed the myths of unrealistic expectations and discover the freedom of being a real mom!

Elisa Morgan and Carol Kuykendall
for MOPS International

Real Moms . . .

- A real mom goes potty with an audience.
- A real mom considers McDonald's a basic food group.
- A real mom uses baby wipes to clean more than dirty bottoms.
- A real mom drives her kids to school in her pajamas.
- A real mom doesn't mind when her kids eat food off the floor; they pick up extra fiber that way.
- A real mom uses her shirt sleeves as napkins and Kleenex.
- A real mom picks up the pacifier that has fallen on the grocery floor, licks it off, and gives it back to her fussy toddler.
- A real mom sometimes accidentally brushes her teeth with hemorrhoid ointment after an incredibly long day with two children under the age of three.
- A real mom allows others to see that she doesn't "have it all together."
- A real mom is just like you and me.

The Myths of Motherhood

> Real is something we become gradually, as we face life vulnerably, returning to God over and over and finding ourselves loved, even when life hurts, when it does not make sense, when we are angry or afraid.
>
> —Brenda Waggoner

Once upon a time, a mother was born.

Though she'd dreamed about becoming a mom for years, her dream became a reality the instant she held her baby in her arms for the first time. Ohhh, she'd been imagining how that tender moment would feel. She'd heard descriptions and seen new moms on television shows crying and making utterances of great joy as they gazed adoringly at their precious little babies. Obviously they felt overwhelmed by waves of intoxicating, pure maternal love. After all, *good moms instantly feel a powerful bonding love for their babies.*

Yet reality surprised her. She eagerly took her baby into her arms—this stranger she had longed to meet—and put her face close to his. She touched his perfect little ears and ran her fingers over his petal-soft skin. His head, misshapen a bit from the birthing process, was topped by a mass of dark curly hair. (Where did that come from? she wondered.) As she looked into his murky grey eyes, she felt a stirring of unfamiliar, tangled emotions deep inside her. Love, yes, but also an odd kind of fear and self doubt. *Who are you, my child? Will I know how to love you for a whole lifetime? Will I be a good mom?*

"Isn't he beautiful?" her own mother cooed, peering at this new grandchild she'd traveled halfway across the continent to greet.

"He is . . ." the new mother agreed. (Of course he looked beautiful to someone who'd traveled so far on so little sleep.)

In her first night at home with her newborn, the new mom faced other surprises.

The baby cried at 2 A.M., and she lovingly fed him. Then she changed him. Then she burped him. Then she patiently rocked him and tried to feed him some more. But an hour later, he was still fussing, and she felt fatigued and frustrated. *Good moms instinctively know what their babies need, so moms who don't must be incompetent.*

A few minutes later, her mother appeared at the bedroom door. "Let me take him into my room for the rest of the night so you can get some sleep, honey," she offered.

"Thanks, but I'm doing okay," the new mom said, because she knew that *good moms sacrifice themselves for their children, joyfully and selflessly, and don't ask for help from others.*

A few days later, her mom packed up to go home. Before leaving, she loaded the refrigerator with groceries, vacuumed and cleaned the living room, and changed all the sheets. The new mom sat in a chair in the living room, feeding the baby, while her husband loaded grandma's luggage in the car for the trip to the airport. Her mom hugged and kissed the two of them goodbye, wiping away a tear as she told them she loved them. And then she was gone. As the car pulled out of the driveway, the new mom started crying. Why was she feeling so sad and alone? After all, *good moms are totally fulfilled and satisfied with their lives as mothers, and they don't complain.*

This new mom had been a mom for only a few days, but already she was beginning to realize that the real world she'd entered was not exactly the picture-perfect world she'd expected. Her real-life experiences kept bumping into her good-mom assumptions and expectations. Suddenly there was a disconnect between reality and the image she thought she should live up to. What kind of mother would she be in this bumpy place?

On the one hand, living within the myths of mothering looked attractive. She longed for the apparently simple happiness assumed in those mythical expectations. Reality seemed so disappointing, and well . . . real. On the other hand, the myths, while appearing more appealing on the surface, created exhausting standards to live up to all the time. Wouldn't she feel more honest and relieved to be real?

What was the answer? Myth or reality? Which would be the way to "happily ever after?"

Welcome to the reality of motherhood—a bumpy, wonderful, self-revealing, growing place where a woman faces the constant tension between expectations and reality. Between good-mom myths and real-mom truths.

Okay . . . now we're talking. Every one of us trips over the new-mom realities as we enter motherhood. It's not always the pink-and-blue-edged dream we imagined. Ever been peed in the face by a newborn baby boy? You know what we mean. Okay, so you had a girl; how about mustard-filled diapers?

Sure there are great moments of utter wonder. But not every moment fits our mythical expectations, and neither do our responses; we're way more human than we thought we'd be.

Relax. This is normal. The tension between myth and reality has been going on for eons. The word myth comes from *mythology*, used by the ancient Greeks to describe why things happened when they didn't have a clue. Like what caused lightning or sunrises and sunsets. People believed these myths—explanations—simply because everyone around them repeated them. People did not question whether they were true; they became accepted as truth out of habit. In fact, social scientists today still study how myths shape human behavior.

The same is true with good-mom myths, which are passed down from experienced moms to wanna-be moms or new moms. From mothers-in-law to daughters-in-law. From sappy Mother's Day cards and Mother's Day sermons to the world of mothers at large. These myths stay mysteriously hidden in our hearts and souls until . . . wham! Reality hits, and we face choices. What will we believe—myth or reality?

What if we choose to believe the myth?

Certainly that's an easy and tempting choice, because good-mom myths are natural extensions of the many good-girl myths we've grown up pretending to believe. *Good girls should act like good girls. Good girls are not overly assertive or aggressive. Good girls don't say bad words. Good girls are nice to everyone. Good girls don't get out-loud angry.*

No wonder we little girls have grown into women who have learned to hide our feelings from ourselves and others. We learn to pretend. "How are you?" someone asks. "Fine," we respond automatically, not willing to honestly say that we feel lonely or depressed or afraid at the moment. Most of us pretend that we don't hurt as much as we really do. Or that what we have satisfies more than it really does. We often hide behind carefully constructed masks such as these:

Mask of Happiness: like the mom who puts on a happy face and smiles on the outside, even while she's churning on the inside, because she doesn't always like being a mother, and she doesn't even always like her children. Yet admitting her unhappiness might make her look like a failure or a bad mom. *After all, good moms are happy moms.*

Mask of Busyness: like the mom who takes on more activities and signs up for more school projects and heads up more committees because busyness makes her feel valuable and keeps her from facing the reality of her self-esteem issues. *After all, good moms do it all.*

Mask of Silence: like the mom who decides to say nothing to her family about her need for their help, because she doesn't want to run the risk of irritating them. *After all, good moms keep everyone happy.*

Mask of Denial: like the mom who denies that her child is having a serious problem in school because *good moms have good children,* and she doesn't want to admit her fears about her child's possible deep needs.

Hiding behind a mask doesn't make the feelings or the realities go away. A mask is a mask. It only covers up the feelings—and the realities. They're still there. There's a better way. Replace the masks and myths with truth. Truth frees us to be real.

That's a promise, passed down by Jesus in a single sentence, that not only appears in the Bible but also has been inscribed on the doors of a zillion institutions of higher learning: "You will know the truth, and the truth will set you free" (John 8:32).

Free to quit trying to be so good all the time.

Free to acknowledge that there are no perfect families in this world, and no perfect children and no perfect mothers.

Free to admit where we fall short of our own expectations or someone else's.

Free not to feel guilty about not being good enough or home enough or fun enough or patient enough.

Free to become all God created us to be.

But (and this is an important "but!") the truth does not set us free to be rotten moms. Or give us license to be rude or selfish. Or insensitive and uncaring. Or to stay stuck where we are rather than to grow and stretch toward what we can be.

So where does that leave us in the effort to replace myths with truth and to be more real?

Here's a summary.

Good-mom myths pressure us to be something we can't be and don't need to be, something beyond what we were intended to be. The truth sets us free to be honest and growing and vulnerable.

Good-mom myths fill us with impossible "I shoulds." Truth allows us to focus on the "I ams."

Good-mom myths give us idealistic formulas and unrealistic expectations from a "once upon a time" and "happily ever after" perfect world of make-believe. But we don't live there. We are imperfect people living in the midst of imperfect relationships, trying to do our best, while juggling busy schedules on PMS and bad hair days. In the midst of this reality, we can discover personal growth and contentment as we seek to know the truth and to act like we believe the truth. That takes hard work and sometimes feels risky, but the results are worth the effort.

It's time to explode the myths of motherhood with truth that will set you free to be the best mom you can be. This book will show you the way.

What is a Real Mom?
(And What isn't)

Being real is . . .
- discovering who you are and being who you are.

- knowing what matters most in mothering.

- determining what's most important in your season of life.

- trying to do what is most important and right, not just what feels the best at the moment.

- recognizing the difference between *good* shoulds and *bad* shoulds. (Good should: "I should try to stop yelling at my children." Bad should: "I should be able to keep my children happy.")

Being real is not . . .
- giving up on growing and changing as a person.

- being selfish or self-centered.

- thinking your way is the right and only way.

- being rude or rotten or inconsiderate of others' feelings or needs.

Being real is risky. It is hard work. It is a life-long process.

Real Moms . . .

- A real mom feels an enormous gulf between the mother she would like to be and the mother she perceives herself to be.

- A real mom picks her kids' noses.

- A real mom sometimes takes showers for the sole purpose of being able to cry—very hard—if need be.

- A real mom puts dirty socks on her kids when the clean ones run out.

- A real mom has moments when she wishes she wasn't a mom.

1

Myths about Me

Chapter 1

Real Me Mom

Real Moms Know and Accept Who They Are

> You never find yourself until you face the truth.
> —Pearl Bailey

Myth: A good mom fits a good-mom mold.

Reality: A real mom accepts herself as she is.

Some moms throw big, blow-out-all-the-stops birthday parties for their kids and actually love all the noise and mess and bedlam. Other moms take the birthday child and a friend to a movie and then out to Chuck E. Cheese's.

Some moms can't hold back the tears on their child's first day of preschool. Others celebrate by treating themselves to a tall caramel frappachino with extra caramel.

Some moms love to spend the evening curled up on the couch, reading books to their kids. Other moms take their children for a walk under the starry skies.

Some moms dress their children in perfectly matched outfits. Other moms let their children dress themselves and don't care much about who wears what.

Moms are different, right?

Duh!

We accept this statement, but somehow a myth has been floating around that a good-mom mold exists somewhere out there, and that something is wrong with us if we don't fit it.

Who invented this good-mom mold and gave it power to control our lives? Answer this question for yourself. Your mother? Your mother-in-law? The perfect mother in your neighborhood? The nasty little negative voice in your head? All of the above?

Nobody really knows the origin of the good-mom mold. Remember, it's a mythical mold. But we sure do know what it looks like, and all too familiar is the pressure we feel to fit within its edges.

The good-mom mold contains sweet-sounding, unrealistic expectations like:

- Good moms keep their children's baby books up to date.
- Good moms prepare nutritionally balanced meals for their families, including legumes.
- Good moms provide an age-appropriate, well-stocked creative-activity corner in their family room.
- Good moms clip savings coupons, file them by product type, and remember to take them when they shop.

Blah! Blah! Blah!

Who can live up to such myths? And what a dangerous attempt it would be!

Newsweek columnist Anna Quindlen writes of the damage done by motherhood myths. She remembers a cross-stitched sampler hanging on a pediatrician's wall in her early years of motherhood that read, "God could not be everywhere, so he made mothers." While admitting that such a sentiment is nice, Quindlen holds that it is also dangerous. "The insidious cult of motherhood is summed up by the psychic weight of the sampler on that doctor's wall. We are meant to be all things to small people."[1]

We can see what feeds this myth about a common mold. Moms share lots of similarities. For instance, with the birth of their first child, all moms seem to automatically start speaking the same universal baby-talk language in the same high-pitched tone. All lament about lack of sleep. All seek the safest car seats or most educational toys. All want to be the best moms they can be. Advertising campaigns reinforce this myth of sameness. Don't we all want our children to be healthy and happy? Then why wouldn't we all want to buy the same brand of strained peas or the same diapers?

But the truth is moms are different. We each have different God-given personalities and a history of different life experiences that not only shape who we are but also shape our unique style of mothering. And instead of getting tangled up in the myth that we should all fit the same good-mom mold, real moms embrace their uniqueness. They *know* who they are and *accept* who they are, so they can *be* who they are. With comfortable confidence. As Charles Swindoll writes, "I have begun to realize that secure, mature people are best described in fifteen words. They know who they are . . . they like who they are . . . they are who they are. They are real."[2]

To understand this journey to becoming a Real Me Mom, let's look at both knowing yourself and accepting yourself. Knowing yourself focuses on your identity. Who are you on the inside or at the core of your soul? This "me" is your real identity, and it is first reached by peeling away the layers of who you are on the outside. Many of those layers have been slapped onto you by others like so many markdowns on the tags at T.J. Maxx. Consider a few:

- *I am what others call me.* Not really. When we become so many titles—Whitney's mom, Mark's wife, Anne's sister, Beth's daughter—we begin to wonder what happened to the "me" we used to know.
- *I am what I do.* I'm an accountant. A mother. A tennis player. Nope. You do what you do. You are who you are.
- *I am what others need me to be.* Not this either. Okay— you're definitely a "need-meeter" in this season of self-sacrifice when much of your time and energy is invested in meeting the needs of others. In the early stages of mothering, you see that your kids are bathed and dressed for school and picked up on time and get their homework done and eat healthy meals. But being a need-meeter isn't who you *are* either. That's still something you *do*.
- *I am my children, my mom, my sister, my friend.* Huh? This layer is about the ways we often get ourselves mixed up with others. Our boundaries blur and at times we can have trouble telling where we end and someone else starts. The closeness of new love in a young marriage can become a blurry "oneness" before couples learn the maturity of "separate but equal" love, in which each offers love from a secure sense of self. At first, our baby is part of us. Eventually, he or she becomes separate, but even in the early years, a dependent child still feels like an extension of us. And don't we all struggle to untangle who we are, separate from our own mothers, as we choose what we want to repeat and what we want to replace in our own mothering? Confusion about finding the me-ness in rela-

tionships is normal for most of us as young women and young moms.

- *I am what I've experienced.* This one's getting a little closer to the real inside me. But this still isn't it. No doubt we've all been shaped by the families in which we grew up. Our parents (or lack of them), our birth order, traumas like death, divorce, or moves all combine to shape us. Schooling and friends also shape us. But these things are still not who we *are*. They are forces and circumstances that have helped define and refine only.

What is your identity—or who are you? Do you still struggle in finding the honest answer to that question? For sure, your identity is made up of the outer labels you wear, what you do day in and day out, what you've inherited from your parents, what you've experienced in life, and how you negotiate the vital relationships with people in your days. But at the very core of your inmost being, your identity is determined by the God-given imprints in your soul.

> **At the very core of your inmost being, your identity is determined by the God-given imprints in your soul.**

Here's the description of your true identity, based on God's promises: I am a child of God, uniquely created by him. I am a one-of-a-kind masterpiece, knit together by God in my mother's womb. I have a God-given temperament and certain strengths and weaknesses that influence how I respond to life and to other people. I might be naturally shy or naturally outgoing. I might be a take-charge leader or a more quiet follower. I might like predictable schedules or prefer more spontaneous activities. These qualities aren't graded on a scale of good or not so good. They simply make up who I am, and God wants me to recognize and celebrate and use these traits in my life and the lives of those around me. Especially as a mother!

To understand more about your personality and to identify your uniqueness, you can take one of the many personality tests, such as the Myers-Briggs Type Indicator, that will help you understand whether you are more extroverted or introverted; more of a thinking or feeling person; whether you acquire information through sensing or intuition; and whether you orient toward the outer world with a judging attitude or a perceptive process. All of these traits come out in the way you mother.

Becoming a Real Me Mom begins with knowing your identity: who you are on the *inside*. The second part comes in accepting and being the "inside you" on the outside, which can be difficult because we often care more about whether others accept us than we do about accepting ourselves. So we unwittingly widen the gulf between who we are on the inside and the person we show the world on the outside. As Blaise Pascal put it, "We strive continually to adorn and preserve our imaginary self, neglecting the true one!"

This is a process that starts in childhood, when young girls especially learn to give up parts of who they are to be accepted. In her classic book *Reviving Ophelia*, sociologist Mary Pipher concludes that adolescent girls face the loss of their real selves to gain acceptance in a world in which Barbie Doll looks mesh with Princess Diana grace and Supreme Court Justice Sandra Day O'Connor smarts.

The strategy of acceptance is the process of knowing and accepting this "inside me" with enough confidence to be that person on the outside, and to mother out of that confidence.

Television's Mister Rogers is an unlikely source of some help here. For a third of a century, this minister—child psychologist has strolled into his TV living room, hung up his jacket, and put on his red sweater, replaced his street shoes with sneakers, and then patiently shared with his viewers the secrets of being real in life.

On many a day, looking past the Lego-littered carpet, mothers of young children have absorbed the words of Mister Rogers into their parched souls.

> It's you, I like.
> It's not the things you wear,
> It's not the way you do your hair,
> But it's you, I like!

His words may sound corny and out of sorts in our era of contemporary savvy. But they also seem to soothe a spot of throbbing need. Maybe that's because they echo God's feelings about us. God clearly knows both the inside and the outside me and accepts them both!

> O LORD, you have searched me
>   and you know me.
> You know when I sit and when I rise;
>   you perceive my thoughts from afar.
> You discern my going out and my lying down;
>   you are familiar with all my ways.
> Before a word is on my tongue
>   you know it completely, O LORD. . . .
> For you created my inmost being;
>   you knit me together in my mother's womb.
> I praise you because I am fearfully and wonderfully made;
>   your works are wonderful,
>   I know that full well.
>
> *Psalm 139:1–4; 13–14*

A Real Me Mom knows she is a unique creation. She knows she is an imperfect, fallible human being with both strengths and weaknesses, who is in process, and she recognizes where she needs to grow. She accepts who she is and is committed to being who she is by constantly narrowing the gap between the inside me and the outside me. For example, a shy, quieter mother accepts her introversion instead of trying to be Mrs. Congeniality when her kids' friends come over. She is committed to being on the outside who she is on the inside, because she knows she is loved unconditionally.

Inside and out—real moms replace the myth that moms should fit some mythical good-mom mold with the truth that they are unique. They know who they are; they accept who they are; and they are free to be who they are. They don't try to match some good-mom mold. Ah . . . what a relief.

Who Am i?

Who you are shapes how you mother. Do you know who you are? Many personality tests help you identify your personality, but most are based on four main categories, which have to do with the way we most comfortably and naturally relate to others, get energized and gather information, make decisions, and adapt a lifestyle. Everyone falls into one or the other column in each of these four categories, so choose the description that best fits you.

Introverted Person	versus	Extroverted Person
Likes quiet for concentration		Likes to have people around
Listens more than talks		Talks more than listens
Has trouble remembering names		Is good at greeting people
Thinks before acting		Often acts quickly, sometimes without thinking

Feeling Person versus	Thinking Person
Tends to be very aware of other people and their feelings	Prefers organizing information in a logical, objective way
Dislikes telling people unpleasant things	Feels rewarded when a job is well done
Makes decisions with one's heart	Makes decisions impersonally
Enjoys pleasing others	Task-oriented

Intuitive Person versus	Sensing Person
Likes solving new problems	Dislikes new problems
Dislikes doing the same thing over and over again	Likes established routines
Gets impatient with routine details	Is patient with routine details
Works in bursts of energy	Works steadily, methodically

Perceptive Person versus	Judging Person
Adapts easily to changing situations	Prefers life to be decisive
Sometimes has trouble making decisions	Decide things quickly
Likes to start things	Likes to finish one project at a time
Flexible and spontaneous	Organized, likes things planned

For more on personality tests, do a search on the internet, using the words "personality type tests." You will find sample questions and tests to take. The most common tests are the Myers-Briggs, the Keirsey Temperament Sorter, and Florence Littauer's Personality Plus tests. You could also look at John Trent's test based on four animals—lion, beaver, otter, and golden retriever—which is explained in *What Every Mom Needs* by Elisa Morgan and Carol Kuykendall in the chapter "Identity."

Real Mom Story

"The Real Me" by Elisabeth K. Corcoran

I didn't like being a mother today. And I'm not talking about simply being frustrated. It was one thing after another with both of my kids. And I believe I outright said at one point (under my breath), "I want to give up mothering permanently."

Could this be PMS? *Possibly.* Could it have been circumstantial? *Maybe.* Could I have been tired? *Perhaps.* Have I neglected spending time with God lately? *Conceivable.* Are any of these excuses my point? *Nope.*

I have this feeling more times than I want to admit—mothering does not come naturally to me. I almost feel as if I should confess this to God and ask for forgiveness. And sometimes I do. Because I feel guilty. It doesn't feel right. It doesn't feel like something I should be feeling. But I *do* feel this way. This ache. This "I have so many things I want to do with my life (but I can't quite yet because I'm a mother)" feeling that haunts me at times.

And I felt for so long that I couldn't even utter these words out loud. What kind of woman and mother would I be if I didn't always particularly even *like* being a mother? Well, I figured, since there's nothing new under the sun, that also goes for my feelings. Chances are I am not the first woman in the world to feel this way, to feel this at-times detachment, this intangible longing, this indescribable discontentment. At least, I hope I'm not.

I have this theory. There are three kinds of women. There's the woman who has always known (like, from birth) that she has wanted to be a mother, and she is fantastic at it, thriving in this role. (In fact, for her, it's not a role; it is who she is to the core.) On the other end of the spectrum is the woman who (also, almost

Myths about Me

from birth) has always known that she did *not* want to be a mother, and she finds her womanly fulfillment in a myriad of other ways throughout her life. Then there's the other one in the middle somewhere, the one who wants to be a mom but is the kind that does not automatically love all children. (She loves hers completely and cares infinitely for the children of her friends and extended family, but that's about the extent of it.) For her, mothering is amazing but is not necessarily the defining factor in her life. I have always candidly believed I have fallen into the middle category. I love my kids, but this mothering thing sort of rubs me the wrong way sometimes. Requiring much more selflessness than I ever would have guessed and much more than I seem to have at my disposal to dole out. I have these longings—to do so much more, to be so much more—a longing to still be the one being taken care of, instead of the consummate caregiver.

Yes, I have dreams. Some can wait for me and my season of life to change. And some will not. Yes, I have yearnings and discontentments that drive me to question my commitment to my children. But something I know for sure: I have been handed two children. God could have chosen a childless life for me. But for whatever reason, he didn't. He, the creator and guide of my life, knew the best goals for my life and the best ways to get me there. And he knows my struggles—inside and out—and he is just waiting for me to hand them back over to him.

And so that is what I must do. Do the next thing, take the next step, wake up the next day and meet my children's needs. All the while allowing my God to walk with me and bring me closer to what he wants me to be, which technically should be my ultimate goal and dream anyway. So I'll chase after that dream, the one that can be attained, no matter the season of life.

Reality Check

1. John Calvin once said, "There are only two things you must know—God, and yourself." Which do you know better? How can you get to know the other better?

2. In "The Real Me" story, the author, Elisabeth K. Corcoran, describes three kinds of moms and is *really* honest about which one she is. How does this make you feel? If you are really honest, which type of mom are you?

3. Describe some of the layers that make up the outside you. If you are what you have experienced in life, describe who you are today.

4. Describe who you are on the most inside part of your soul. How well do you accept who you are on the inside? Explain.

5. Where are the differences between who you are on the inside and who you are on the outside? How wide is the gap? How could you narrow this gap?

6. Knowing who we are on the inside is sometimes really hard. Ken Gire writes, "Who we are, who we truly are, is a secret known only to God."[3] God wants to help us know and accept our identity in him. Here are some "I ams" in Jesus. Which do you accept and why?

   I am made in the image of God (Gen. 1:26–27).

   I can grow and change (Phil. 1:6).

   I am a child of God (John 1:12).

For Further Reading

Please Understand Me II: Character and Temperament Types by David Keirsey
The Velveteen Woman by Brenda Waggoner
Inside Out by Larry Crabb
Bravehearts by Sharon Hersh

Real Moms . . .

- A real mom really likes to sleep, but when that sick or scared-from-a-nightmare child only wants Mommy, deep down she really likes that too.
- A real mom doesn't always enjoy Martha Stewart and "all things crafty."
- A real mom never forgets her baby's birth weight but can't remember her own phone number.
- A real mom drinks Coke, even for breakfast if necessary!
- A real mom wonders sometimes if she's really cut out for this job while at the same time wouldn't trade it for the world!

Chapter 2

Perma-Guilt Mom

Real Moms Feel Guilty

> You may feel guilty about leaving your children for your work and guilty about leaving your work for your children. You will no doubt also feel guilty about feeling guilty.
>
> —Harriet Lerner

Myth: A good mom doesn't feel guilty.

Reality: A real mom knows guilt is a permanent part of her life.

You thought you'd never mush all the colors of Play-Doh together in one can, but you did just that earlier today. You don't know much about the family you just dropped your child off to play with for the afternoon. Though you swore you wouldn't give in to your child's whining in the grocery line, you just purchased a big bag of Skittles to get through the checkout peacefully. And worst of all, you pretended to look the other way when a box of sugar-coated cereal landed in your cart. Now it's in your bag, and soon it will be in your pantry and on your kitchen table. As you maneuver your way out of the parking lot, the layers of guilt settle over you.

The truth is out for all to see: you're a lousy mother. Or so you believe, because "good" moms don't fail so often or feel so much guilt. They do FBI-rated background checks on the neighbors' kids before allowing any playtime at all. They carefully monitor their child's daily intake of sugar. And they *always* sterilize the baby's pacifier, even if she's the third child in the family. (True confession: you've recently taken to wiping it off on your jeans when it falls to the floor.)

But here's the real truth. All moms struggle with a condition called perma-guilt. If something goes wrong, we believe it's our fault. Hardly matters what it is. You name it; we feel guilty about it. Guilty is normal.

This condition of constant guilt seems to have two components. First, there's the responsibility part. Moms feel responsible for the *entire world* of their child. From the second they're conceived to their eventual exodus to college or down the aisle or into a new apartment, the tasks of child-creating and child-rearing are assumed to be the mom's. (Some so-called expert, undoubtedly male, even suggests that a child's woes in life can actually be blamed on "Womb Doom," things like what mom ate or didn't eat—or what she did or didn't do—that doomed the child before he or she was even born.)

Moms see themselves as responsible for everything from what their children eat to what they wear to how they act. Then there's homework and manners and teeth flossing, and the list goes on. Okay, there may be a dad to help out, and he serves a vital role, but if you ask a mom, she'll tell you the buck stops with her. The sense of responsibility is the first burden of the Perma-Guilt Mom.

What's the second part? Well then there's the ability. And here's where the problem really hits the fan. If a mom is responsible for the *entire world* of her child, then she's bound to face a normal fear that she lacks the ability to successfully follow through on all those responsibilities. Who could? One counselor suggests that guilt is the result of feeling responsible for something but not feeling skilled enough to accomplish the requirements. Bingo. Not rocket science here. Moms feel like they have total responsibility but not total ability. That equals guilt!

> **Guilt is the result of feeling responsible for something but not feeling skilled enough to accomplish the requirements.**

Real moms do feel guilt! Perma-guilt! This myth that "good" moms don't feel guilty paralyzes us, and we begin to think we're crazy! As Harriet Lerner puts it in her book *The Mother Dance,* "Guilt keeps mothers narrowly focused on the question, 'What's wrong with me?' and prevents us from becoming effective agents of personal and social change."[1] Instead of mothering from reality, where we realize and accept that we have a limited amount of wisdom and time, we sometimes use up what's left of our energy to mix up and bake batches of "guilt cookies" for our miffed children, all in an attempt to lessen our feelings of perma-guilt.

Making matters even worse, our perma-guilt covers up other emotions that need expression and release. When we peel back the top layer of guilt, we're likely to find anger closely beneath the surface. "Why do people expect me to be totally responsible for the *entire world* of my child?! Who could know how to do all that?" Next comes hurt. "Why didn't someone tell me this would be so hard and that no one else would appreciate what I do? Why isn't my mother a better grandmother? Why doesn't (someone) help me more?" Next is a layer of sadness. "Oh dear, why am I such a bad mom? Why can't I handle this better? What's the matter with me?" Finally, there is the fear. "What if I totally mess up my child? What if it's my fault?"

All too often, others don't try to remove the burden of guilt from our shoulders. Do people think that feeling guilty is good for moms? Or normal? As writer Anne Lamott discovered in her own guilt-ridden mothering, the whole world out there actually wants moms to feel guilty *and* ashamed. After all, won't that make moms try to be better moms?

So what's a mother to do? Good question—with a pretty good answer. First, recognize that moms have needs too. Get real about the guilt. Just because you're the mom and in charge of taking temperatures, making mac and cheese, and creating birthday parties doesn't mean that you don't still have needs yourself. You might have faced this fact. One day when you got the flu, you woke up to the reality that you're still a human who has a stop button along with a go button.

Like many moms, you may be living under the myth that your needs aren't as important as everyone else's and are feeling guilty about meeting your own needs. We know that we need sleep, some exercise, like a run through the neighborhood or a swim at the Y, time alone in the bathroom for a bath or whatever, lunch out with the girls, and a date night now and then.

We like the way psychologists Henry Cloud and John Townsend illustrate the flaws of this myth in their book *Twelve Christian Beliefs That Can Drive You Crazy*. The first chapter, called "It's Selfish to Have My Needs Met," tells this story:

Picture yourself at a gas station. Your car is on empty and you are in the middle of a long journey. You step out of your car, walk around to the pump, grab the nozzle, and shove it into your tank. Just as you're ready to swipe your credit card and punch "start," someone from the next pump approaches you. "Hey, how come you're filling up your tank when I'm on empty? And look at that teenager over there; she's on empty. There's a mother whose kids are younger than yours right behind you, and she's on empty too. Aren't you a selfish one! You ought to be filling up all their tanks first. What are you doing filling up your own?"[2]

Hmm. Aren't we the selfish ones? Subtle question, yes, but completely stifling; this mothering myth brainwashes us into believing that we'd better hold off on meeting our own needs because that's what good mothers do. And not even acknowledging our needs is even more mature.

Ready to get real about your needs? Answer this question: What do you need in order to do what God has given you to accomplish in your family during this season of your life? In your community? In your world?

You are in charge of your self-care, and when real moms accept the important responsibility of getting that care, they have more to offer their kids, their families, and the world around them. You can't give what you don't have. Being selfish enough to meet your own most important needs as a mom is the very thing that helps you meet the needs of those you love. Some guilt will be there no matter what.

Second, learn to distinguish between two kinds of guilt: good guilt and not-so-good guilt. Then you can learn to deal with it.

Good guilt is the kind of guilt that slides up your spine and gently nudges you on the shoulder. "Get a grip here!" it whispers. "You don't need to take your bad mood out on your eighteen-month-old. It's not her fault you have cramps, or haven't eaten anything today, or might get laid off from your job." Good guilt opens the doors to healing and helps in those places where we need to grow and change. We have to see—really see—our need for help from others and from God before we can receive it. Good guilt shines the light of truth on our wrong ways so that we can recognize our mistakes and see our way toward change.

Getting to the Bottom of Guilt

Moms feel guilty. Yet guilt is like a blanket that often covers other feelings. Here are descriptions of the layers that might be lurking below your guilty feelings. If you honestly answer these questions, you might get to the bottom of your feelings.

First Layer: Guilt

- Am I spending enough time with my kids?
- Am I yelling at them more than I should?
- Am I disciplining them properly?

These are the kinds of questions we commonly ask ourselves—and feel guilty with our answers. But lurking just below this layer of guilt may be something else.

Second Layer: Anger

- Who might I be angry with?
- What might I be angry at?
- Why would I feel angry?

These questions help you identify an underlying anger. But anger often covers up hurt. So move on down to that layer of feelings.

Third Layer: Hurt

- Do I feel hurt about something?
- Why do I feel hurt?
- What part of me feels threatened or not valued?
- What can I do with this hurt?

Fourth Layer: Fear

- What am I afraid of?
- Do I have any control over what I'm afraid of?
- What is out of my control that I need to surrender to God?
- How can I turn this fear into a prayer?

Once you get to the bottom of these feelings underneath your guilt, you have some choices. If another person has hurt you, you can go to that person and talk out your issues. You can seek out the support or encouragement of a friend or counselor. You can get a babysitter and spend some time doing whatever waters and heals the wounded roots of your soul. You can also say a prayer to God about your wounds or your fears. He understands your pain so deeply.

Not-so-good guilt? Well that's the stuff that holds us responsible for the impossible—for things we have no ability to be responsible for. Like whether a child gets sick or grows according to the growth chart. Think of it this way. In 2 Corinthians 7:10, the apostle Paul describes the difference: "Godly sorrow brings repentance that leads to salvation and leaves no regret, but worldly sorrow brings death."

While that sounds heavy, what Paul means is that good guilt leads to healing and growth but not-so-good guilt is deadly and eventually saps the life right out of us. Why? Because not-so-good guilt (worldly sorrow) is a burden that we end up carrying around all day and night. And it keeps getting heavier and heavier. We weren't meant to carry such a weight around.

Moms are going to live with guilt. True. That's part of dealing with the responsibilities of mothering. But real moms find freedom by learning to distinguish between good guilt and not-so-good guilt. We learn where we need to grow and move past the accusations of the impossible. As real moms, we struggle with guilt, but we're not manipulated by it.

"What's a Mom to Do?" by Amy Ridgeway

In the short summer months between school years, amazing things can happen to a child, almost without notice. She somehow progresses from preschooler to student without so much as a backward glance. There she is, sprinting to the finish line of adulthood, with me lagging somewhere behind, gasping for breath, tripping over shoelaces, wondering where the nearest rest stop is and just how I got into this race in the first place.

With all of her six-year-old confidence, she can look at me, who has shopped diligently in accordance with the myriad of lists distributed by the school, and say "You did not buy the right notebook, Mom. My composition book is all wrong, and those aren't the right kind of glue sticks."

If she only knew just how often I will disappoint her, she would save her wrath for the really big things. For example, I did not know that the first day of school was a half-day. Apparently every other good parent did. Fortunately, the bus makes a distinctive sound, and I have a friend—a good mom—who knows when her child will be arriving home, and she doesn't mind clueing me in!

It also occurs to me that my husband's mom does not come over to read him a story before bed every night. So my days of *Rapunzel* and *Harry Dog* may not last forever, even though my child is so very sweet then, all clean and pink from the bath and eagerly listening to my silly voices and sillier tales just minutes before dropping off to sleep. Nor will I always be able to please her with the good kind of macaroni and cheese, the kind with that bright orange powder and little noodles shaped like logs that fit perfectly over the tines of a fork.

What's a mom to do? This is not just a rhetorical question. I remember wondering, in the early days of Joanna's infancy, just when the real mom would show up and fill me in (the one who knew what she was doing). I think I'm still looking for her!

Reality Check

1. Repeat to yourself: "I am not responsible for my child's *entire world!* I am responsible for my own life and the choices I make." Do you believe this? How can you begin to own this as a truth?

2. When you feel like you're running on empty, your life is filled with "I can'ts," find some "I cans" for yourself by giving your own examples here:

   - Three things only I *can* do.
     1.
     2.
     3.

     Examples:
       1. Identify my needs.
       2. Take responsibility for my needs.
       3. Ask for help.

   - Three things I *can* ask another person to do.
     1.
     2.
     3.

     Examples:
       1. Spend time with me.
       2. Spend time with my children.
       3. Pray with me and help hold me accountable for my self-care.

Myths about Me

- Three people I *can* ask for help.
  1.
  2.
  3.

- Three ways I *can* have fun.
  1.
  2.
  3.

3. How is good guilt motivating a positive change in your life? In what areas do you need to grow and change?

4. Author Stormie Omartian comments about a mother's guilt: "From the time her children are born or come into her life, a part of *her* is always with *them*."[3] Knowing this is normal, how does this statement release you from the guilt you feel when you are not always with your children?

5. No one can make you feel guilty. You have to decide to feel guilty all for yourself. Do you believe this? Explain.

6. What things do you feel "falsely" guilty about?

7. Dietrich Bonhoeffer said, "Guilt is the idol hardest to break down." What do you think he means? Do you think some of your mistakes are too much for God to forgive? Do you believe you are beyond his forgiveness? Why? What do you think God thinks about your response?

For Further Reading

The Mother Dance by Harriett Lerner
The Mask of Motherhood by Susan Maushart
When I Relax I Feel Guilty by Tim Hansel

Real Moms . . .

- A real mom feels guilty about something everyday.

- A real mom answers the phone sounding like she's out of breath when her husband calls from work.

- A real mom can acknowledge her mistakes with her children, husband, and herself and then take steps to work on making the family work better.

- A real mom can do many jobs at once but never feels she is doing a satisfactory job at any one of them.

- A real mom knows that no matter how many books and articles she reads, no matter how much of her time and energy she gives her kids, she could always do more or should do less.

- A real mom joins a health club not to work out but because she can take an uninterrupted shower while the club's day care watches her kids.

Chapter 3

Monster Mom

Real Moms Get Angry

> One of the worst things about being a parent, for me, is the self-discovery, the being face to face with one's secret insanity and brokenness and rage.
>
> —Anne Lamott

Myth: A good mom is nice and patient all the time.

Reality: A real mom gets angry.

You know her. She's the one standing in the middle of the family room, face red, eyes wide, fists clenched closed, kid-clutter strewn around her feet. Her pulse is racing. Her mouth is dry. Her teeth clutch the tip of her tongue, nipping it with warnings, "Stay put! Don't say it!"

She had awakened this Saturday morning with the vow that this was going to be a "good mommy" day. No yelling. Lots of patience. All day long. Five minutes ago she was enjoying a cup of coffee and the morning newspaper. She assumed her two-year-old twins were quietly watching cartoons. So far so good. Then she experienced that all too familiar, uneasy mom-moment when she suddenly knew it was too quiet. She put down the paper and hurried into the family room. And stared in horror at the sight. There, on the wall above the couch, were bold, colorful crayon markings in huge random scribblings. Two cherub-faced toddlers turned, a crayon in each hand, and greeted her with gleeful grins. "For you, Mommy. Pretty, Mommy?"

You recognize this mom, don't you? Her hair is standing on end, her thoughts churning as she searches for words, for her voice, for a sound, and suddenly she erupts, "What do you think you're doing! Crayons are not for the wall! They are for paper! That paper there on the table!"

You know her—and the rest of the story.

What's that? You say you don't recognize this mom? You're kidding. You do so. This is Monster Mom. Surely you know her because she lives inside all us moms.

What? You still say you don't know her? Well maybe you call her by another name. Momzilla? Mom-Attack Mamma? Volcanic Mom? Screaming Meemy Mommy?

Oh come on, admit you know her. Seriously. Why do you insist that moms don't get angry? You're in denial. YOU'RE LYING! THEY DO SO! QUIT PRETENDING! *Hey . . . admit it . . . you know monster mom really well cuz she lives inside you too, and at this very second, she's ready to pounce or growl or escape so she can come out and be recognized!*

Ohhh. Sorry about that angry outburst. It's just really hard to pretend that there's no such thing as Monster Mom. Sure, we might like to believe that moms never get angry, that they're nice and patient all the time. But this, like so many other ideas, is a myth. Real moms do get angry. They get impatient and snarly and lose it with their own children. Or they get icy silent, pulled-away, shut in on themselves, seething at everyone. And sometimes they don't even like their kids.

Now admit this is too true, even for you. And sit back and let some of this reality sink in. The truth makes us all better moms, especially where anger is concerned.

> **it's just really hard to pretend that there's no such thing as Monster Mom.**

Moms have an unusual battle with anger. It's a lose-lose-lose situation. First lose? Well, in our day and age, anger is plain nasty. It's a negative emotion. It's got a bad reputation. It's messy and ugly and volatile and unpredictable and revealing and emotional.

Second lose? Women aren't supposed to get angry. They're bad if they do. Men can be angry. With them, anger is kind of macho. Out there. Normal testosterone stuff. To be expected. Take road rage, for instance. It's nearly normal for men to show their anger behind the wheel. They honk the horn. Flash their bright lights. But women? No way. An angry woman is seen as a shrew. She's a scary person. She's whacked. She's bad. Women are allowed to be angry only if their anger is indirect. They can feel depressed. Or guilty. Or moody. But not angry.

Third lose? Moving beyond the gender issue is a role issue. *Mothers* should *never* be angry. Oh my goodness, no. An angry mom is a dangerous mom. Abusive. Bungling. Damaging. Horrible. Witch.

Problem here is that moms, more than just about any other category of human beings, are the most likely to battle anger, for many reasons. For one, we live so constantly with moments that are out of our control. Think about it. Your day is planned, but your child gets sick, and so the day has to get unplanned and replanned. Another reason is the fact that motherhood is supposed to be so fulfilling and wonderful and a calling that surely brings out the best in women. Anger in the midst of this high and holy calling is an unaccepted emotion. A final reason for battling anger is the fear that expressing it will ruin our children. (There's a double whammy here, since at times we *can* and *have* caused damage by inappropriately expressing anger in front of our children. Above all, we don't want to do that!)

> **Moms have an unusual battle with anger. it's a lose-lose-lose situation.**

Lose-lose-lose. Of course you don't want to admit that you know Monster Mom! But you do. You know her well. Quite well. She lives in the space behind your eyes. She swirls through your chest. She courses through your veins. And yes, at times, she pops out for an appearance, sometimes clear and rational, other times anything but. Monster Mom is alive and well in the you that is a mom in your home.

We need to get some things straight about anger.

Anger is a neutral feeling. It's neither good nor bad. It's just a feeling. It's what we do with it that can help or hurt. Many of us have been spoonfed the myth that anger is a sin, but the Bible is clear: it is not. When Paul writes to the Ephesians in 4:26, he says, "In your anger do not sin." Clearly, these words acknowledge that we will become angry. What we're to watch out for is what we do when we become angry. That's where sin can come in.

Anger is a normal feeling, a normal human emotion—not a male or female emotion. While our society may *permit* some to express anger and others not to express it, we experience anger equally, whether we are male or female, young or old. But when we try to *avoid* getting angry because we think it's not appropriate, we set ourselves up for trouble, because such expectations are impossible. "I'm not going to lose it today, not even once!" we vow as our feet hit the floor in the morning. Only a half hour later, something sets us off and out of our mouths tumble those ugly angry words we vowed we wouldn't say. Later, we heap guilt on top of our anger. "I was *never* going to act this way!" we wail. Or, "I sound just like my mother, and I swore I *never* would!" When we create impossible expectations for ourselves, we only add fuel to our potential for anger, and our fuse gets shorter!

Anger is usually a secondary feeling. It's usually not the first thing we feel. It's an emotion that comes from another emotion like sadness or hurt or loss or pain or fear or frustration. For moms, stuff like finding crayon pictures on the wall can trigger anger. Or running into a need in our child that we can't meet. Or missing out on the time we'd set aside to be alone and refuel when we know we're running on empty.

Okay. There's something else to acknowledge here. Anger can lead to abuse. It can create cracks in marriages. It can escalate minor everyday struggles into disastrous outcomes. But anger leads to such damaging results only when it is expressed inappropriately. Either explosively or by suppressing it. Both ways are wrong.

At least *explosively* communicates the anger with honesty, even though inappropriately. Suppressing the anger can have even more damaging results. When anger is ignored, denied, and stuffed inside, you can do greater damage, because first of all, you are communicating a lie with your covered-up feelings. Also, your suppressed anger can start coming out in different passive-aggressive ways, such as through sarcasm, nagging, silence, withdrawal, or by taking it out on the wrong person. Or by finally exploding at the right person with emotions that are way out of proportion to the incident at hand.

> **Suppressed anger is anger over which we have little control.**

Suppressed anger is anger over which we have little control. We don't evaluate it or take responsibility for it. Yet when we learn to recognize and direct our anger in appropriate methods, anger remains under our control.

Real moms get angry. At times, we can be Monster Moms. What's important is to learn to recognize and handle anger when it comes.

Here's how:

- *Know your symptoms.* Each mom has her own warning signals regarding anger. The more introverted mom may slowly seethe on the inside, while trying to maintain perfect composure on the outside. Then she starts feeling depressed, or her stomach gets tied in knots. The more extroverted mom may blow on the spot, but her warning signals might be a dry mouth or a heightened pulse or a ringing in her head.
- *Know your style of expression.* Are you the physical type who grabs pots and pans to slam around? Are you a screamer who needs to get it all out quickly and loudly? Or do you tend to get icy quiet and need some time alone to sort things through? When you know your style, you can deal with the results sooner.
- *Know your survival techniques.* Plan a response ahead of time. Find a friend who will agree to rescue you, or your children, at a moment's notice when you reach the end of your rope. Find a place that is safe for your retreat. Give yourself a time-out and lock yourself in the bathroom where you can scream into a towel or punch a pillow. Get out of the house. Go for a walk. Play tennis or jog around the neighborhood. Talk to a friend or your husband. Try to figure out what is beneath your anger: sadness, loss, hurt, pain, or frustration over what you can't control.

Real moms don't stuff their anger. Nor do they erupt like volcanoes. They understand that anger is a normal human emotion, and they work at learning to handle their angry feelings in ways that bring healing and growth and hope to themselves and the people around them.

Real Mom Story

"Momzilla Finds an 'Attitude Adjuster'" by Lisa Moffitt

My three children are little angels most of the time, but there are those days when, from the time they wake up, they are chopping at my nerves like machete-wielding explorers going through an uncharted jungle. It's days like these that make me turn into Momzilla by afternoon. Take Thursday, for instance. It started out with their complaints. "Mom, I don't like Fruit Loops. I want Yucky Charms." I replied, "Sweetie, you ate Fruit Loops yesterday." "I don't like my tennis shoes. I want some with lights." "Honey, you picked those out last week," I replied with a smile.

Then there was the teasing name-calling. As I took a deep breath, I told Jesse that he must apologize to his sister because he shouldn't call people names. Jesse replied with a devilish gleam in his eyes, "I'm sorry, Pee-Pee Head."

After a morning of whining and crying, they decided to play together, finally. Danielle asked me for the magic markers because they were going downstairs to play clowns. *Oh, how creative my little kindergartner has become*, I thought to myself.

Big, huge, gigantic mistake! I should have realized that magic markers and "playing clown" do not mix. The three came up the steps crying and yelling over the blue marker. As I came around the kitchen counter to referee, I saw these multicolored,

Dealing with Anger – and the Aftermath

So much of life revolves around this familiar cycle: We lose it. We yell. We say things we shouldn't. We act in anger. And now we have to deal with the aftermath. We need to apologize. We know it. But there's a simple principle here: the more we practice our response to this cycle, the easier and quicker we can do what we're supposed to do. Here are some steps in dealing with anger, and the aftermath.

Stop. When you feel the anger rising up inside you, stop! Wait. Take a deep breath. Do nothing until you ask yourself, What is this anger about, really? Is it what I'm seeing or feeling, or is it something underneath it? What can I do about it? What is the appropriate response? Remember, your anger is a normal human emotion, but how you express that anger can be right or wrong.

Talk to God. Prayer helps put our feelings into perspective.

Express your feelings appropriately. Act in a way that you won't be sorry for later. But seek to express yourself in some way. Don't continually try to suppress your feelings.

Evaluate your actions. Maybe you blew it. Maybe you yelled. Maybe you acted inappropriately. Maybe you wrongly hurt someone in the process. Maybe you need to say "I'm sorry."

Apologize. Take the initiative and go to the person. Don't wait for that person to come to you. Say "I'm sorry. I acted wrongly. Please forgive me." Sometimes you find those words are surprisingly hard to say, but like the Nike ad encourages, "Just do it!"

Receive forgiveness. A child is so quick to forgive. Receive forgiveness you've asked for and receive the freedom of a burden lifted.

Move on. Evaluating actions, apologizing, and accepting forgiveness opens the door to the miracle of a new beginning. And personal growth. Just like we're told not to hold grudges, we also don't hold on to guilt. It's time to move on. That's part of the cycle.

When I see a symbol of the cross, I think forgiveness. The vertical crossbeam reminds me that through Jesus Christ, God has forgiven me. The horizontal beam tells me that now, as forgiven sinners, we can model Christ's life by forgiving others and seeking their forgiveness.

CHUCK SWINDOLL

white-toothed, raging banshees fighting each other. I tried to breathe, but it was too late. Momzilla had emerged. I could feel her low rumbling growl as she straightened up that last nerve.

Momzilla stomped her way into the kitchen. Dishtowels and houseplants were blowing from the force as she passed by. She picked up her trusty attitude adjuster, otherwise known as a flyswatter, and waved it through the air as she made her way to the den.

All three clown children ran to their rooms yelling, "We won't do it again," as they covered their behinds. Momzilla followed, hot on the trail of tears. Her tongue wagged and loud indecipherable words came from her mouth. Steam poured from her ears as she slapped the flyswatter against her own leg for sound effects.

Momzilla heard the children in the background promising never to be clowns again if Mommy would just come back. Momzilla took a slow deep breath, and then another. As Momzilla returned to the cage that I keep her in, I noticed how cute my little clowns were. And I realized that this was a memory I would remember long after my kids were gone. I also realized that the monster in me was two times worse than the clowns my children had become. I resolved that next time (and there will be a next time), I will do a couple more "deep breathing" exercises during the day. Then, if I still have problems with Momzilla's cage door wanting to explode open, I will separate myself from the situation. "Calgon, take me away!"[1]

Reality Check

1. Anger can be used as a defense to keep us from feeling other even more painful emotions. Think of a recent time when you experienced anger. What do you find when you push past the

anger to the feelings beneath it? How can you help yourself deal with these tender feelings? How can you keep from covering up these feelings in the future?

2. Anger sometimes comes when our space, rights, or feelings of self-worth have been violated. Can you name such a time in the last several weeks? What can you do to deal with your need for space and time and feelings of significance?

3. Sometimes we are more likely to let anger seethe inside of us when we have not processed pain from our own upbringing or from some event in our past. This can cause passive-aggressive behaviors, like hollering at your husband on the phone when you're really mad at your toddler for wetting his pants. Take some time to analyze what experiences, wounds, and tender spots you are bringing into your mothering. These can be triggers to inappropriate expressions of anger. Be gentle with yourself but hold yourself accountable to understand these issues. Pursue a mentoring or counseling relationship if necessary.

4. Mothering is the ultimate reality check. It brings out more of who we are than we would like to see. How does Monster Mom reveal your flaws, bumps, and imperfections as a mom? What does God say is true about you, even in your Monster Mom moments? For what inappropriate moments of anger do you need to ask forgiveness? Are you able to say "I'm sorry" to your children?

5. Next time you feel angry, ask yourself, Why am I angry? What am I going to do with these feelings? How will I express them appropriately?

For Further Reading

She's Gonna Blow! by Julie Ann Barnhill
When You Feel Like Screaming by Pat Holt and Grace Ketterman
The Dance of Anger by Harriet Lerner
Good Women Get Angry by Gary J. Oliver and H. Norman Wright
Why Do I Feel This Way? by Brenda Poinsett

Real Moms...

- A real mom sometimes gets tired, frustrated, and mad at her kids.

- A real mom cries over spilled milk.

- A real mom fusses at her kids a good part of the day, then lingers over them as they sleep.

- A real mom sometimes has bad days (or weeks).

- A real mom says to her kids, "I'm sorry. I was wrong. Will you forgive me?"

Chapter 4

Please Everyone Mom

*Real Moms Can't Fix Everyone
and Everything*

Extravagant love involves learning how to live well
in the midst of chaos, disappointment and miscues.
—Sharon A. Hersh

Myth: A good mom keeps everyone happy.

Reality: A real mom can't fix everyone
and everything.

If mama ain't happy, ain't nobody happy.

Really?

In your family, who is supposed to be responsible for attitudes, moods, atmosphere—*life!?* Who is the chairman in charge of cheerfulness? Who monitors the controls that regulate the family's feelings? Who is the peacemaker? Who assumes responsibility to make sure that all the stuff of life is neat and tidy and Christian and clear? The answer? Mom!

Guess what? Moms can't please everyone. They can't keep life neat and tidy. Life is messy. People aren't always happy. X doesn't always lead to Y. The sun doesn't always come out. Kids don't always obey. (In fact, they often learn more when they don't.) People get cancer. Planes fly into buildings. Unexpected crises happen. We're not in charge. Or in control. Sadness is as real in our lives as joy.

And moms can't always fix everyone and everything.

Why would we believe this myth and think we could or should in the first place? Probably for a couple of reasons. There's a part of us that *wants* to make everybody happy because that makes us happy. We like being valued for solving sticky problems, and we like feeling loved by our children (which happens most when they're happy). When our kids are grouchy and creepy, we end up feeling grouchy, creepy, unsuccessful—and unloved. So why wouldn't we work hard at keeping everybody happy to get this positive feedback?

A toddler waiting impatiently in a pediatrician's office begins to lose it, so his mom pulls a surprise out of her purse. Presto: good mood change! Good mom! A child whines. He might be tired, but we assume he's acting out against us or that we should have foreseen his need to nap or that it's up to us to help him work through his mood. So we work hard to help him get back a good attitude. Good mom! What would happen if we didn't intervene? Bad moods! Bad mom?

Besides our need for positive feedback, another reason we take on attitude control in our families comes from how we were made and how we were raised. The desire to help and fix and

> **Guess what? Moms can't please everyone. They can't keep life neat and tidy. Life is messy. People aren't always happy. X doesn't always lead to Y. The sun doesn't always come out. Kids don't always obey.**

make peace is not a new assumed responsibility for women. Decades ago, Anne Morrow Lindbergh, wife of the famous aviator, wrote these words about a woman's fears of spilling herself away as she fulfills her responsibilities: "All her instinct as a woman—the eternal nourisher of children, of men, of society—demands that she give. Her time, her energy, her creativeness drain out into these channels if there is any chance, any leak. Traditionally we are taught, and instinctively we long, to give where it is needed—and immediately. Eternally, woman spills herself away in driblets to the thirsty, seldom being allowed the time, the quiet, the peace, to let the pitcher fill up to the brim."[1]

> **While uniquely gifted to nurture, moms are often crippled by a desire to please.**

While uniquely gifted to nurture, moms are often crippled by a desire to please. In plain language, this is called codependency, and there isn't anything pretty about it. The truth is this: if mama ain't happy, it's her responsibility to deal with it, nobody else's. And if anybody else ain't happy, it's not mama's fault or problem. It's theirs.

Accepting this reality requires us to understand the need for boundaries in our lives and in the lives of others. In their bestselling book *Boundaries,* Dr. Henry Cloud and Dr. John Townsend write, "Boundaries define us. They define *what is me* and *what is not me*. A boundary shows me where I end and someone else begins."[2]

In other words, boundaries help you know what belongs to you and what doesn't. Thinking of boundaries in a physical form helps us understand this vital concept. Boundaries define a person's property line, invisible but real, pointing out what you own and what you don't. They let you know what you are and are not responsible for.

For example, the Bible talks about "carrying each other's burdens" in Galatians 6:2, but that doesn't mean to lay down your own load and pick up another's. Nor are we to heap another's on top of ours. What God is calling us to do is understand whose burden belongs to whom; to take up our *own* load as our *own;* and to reach out in assistance when possible, coming alongside others as they carry their loads. In fact, that's how that part of the passage ends: "Each one should test his own actions. Then he can take pride in himself, without comparing himself to somebody else, for each one should carry his own load" (vv. 4–5).

All this means that we should not be codependent. We should recognize our boundaries, accept our own responsibilities, and let our children do the same. But that can be hard work because we have to discern the difference between myth and reality and to live out the truth. The question is this: If it's simply impossible for moms to *please* others, what *can* we do?

Stop trying to fix everyone and everything! Accept that life is messy. And we have to start by looking at ourselves. We won't always be happy or content. We won't always like our kids. Sometimes we may even wish they weren't our kids. Likewise, our kids aren't always going to like us. We won't always be there to protect or intervene or fix or correct or make peace. Their problems are not our problems, and we need to resist the temptation to let them become our problems. Though we can sympathize, express understanding, and validate their feelings, we can't fix or control their moods. We need to recognize the stuff in our own lives that make or break our own moods and deal with those issues. Life is messy—even ours. And that's okay.

This is especially tough for moms when we've become a bit dependent on our kids to make us feel good. See, when we need our kids to be happy so we'll be happy, or to love us so we'll feel loved, it's pretty hard to confront them or deprive them or withhold something from them, in short, to discipline them. Understand? Because then our child might not give us what we think we need, and we'll have to get our needs met another way. Hmm. And we may not know how to do that.

Now, once again, being real isn't license to be rotten. Nobody wants a grumpy, gritchy, or complaining martyr mom. So when we're in one of those moods, it's up to us to recognize how we're going to deal with ourselves—when and how we need a break or need to grow, need a friend, or need therapy in order to be the best moms we can possibly be.

One mom came up with a creative way of dealing with her grumpy mood as Mother's Day approached one year. She was disappointed in the way her family celebrated that day, because they hardly did. So as she wandered through a shopping mall, bombarded with reminders of Mother's Day gifts, she knew she could go home grumpier and wallowing in self pity about their attitudes, or she could take charge of her own attitude—and celebration. So she popped into a store, got a small gift for each of her children, and on Mother's Day, she presented those gifts, thanking her children for making her a mom.

We start by taking charge of ourselves, and then we move on to our kids. As real moms, we help our children learn to take responsibility for their own messiness in life—bad moods, unfair circumstances, and other realities. Taking responsibility means learning the ability to respond to this messiness, and kids learn that best when we moms don't step in and assume those responsibilities for them. Otherwise, all we'll do is reinforce the connected myths that (1) life is always happy and there's something wrong if you're not happy all the time, and that (2) if you're not happy, mom will be there to fix it. Or we teach our children to play the blame game, always blaming someone or something else for their bad moods.

Psychologist John Rosemond warns us, "Child-centered moms expect a lot of themselves. Consequently, their children, instead of respecting them, expect of them."[3]

Moms do assume a major responsibility when their children are young, however. And it's a tough one. It's called containment, which is the "mothering function where the mom literally *keeps* the child's feelings until he can handle them for himself."[4] In the early years, children are not able to handle their emotions of love and hate and fear and sadness, for instance. So the mother "takes in and holds on to these feelings . . . and gradually feeds them back to the child in a way that he can digest them without being overwhelmed by them. In this way, she prepares the child for taking responsibility for his feelings when he has matured sufficiently."[5] For a mom, containment involves holding their anger and even the dreaded words "I hate you!" The challenge is to remain calm and simply contain the emotions without taking responsibility for them, or getting angry in return.

Are you kidding? Hearing "I hate you!" and remaining calm? Isn't that *way* disrespectful? Could be. What this really means is allowing your child to respond to the truth that life is messy with his or her honest emotions. (Remember, Monster Mom, anger is a neutral feeling. It's what we *do* with it that can be good or bad.)

Okay—so all of this sounds ridiculously hard and maybe even incredulous to the mom who has an easy three-year-old who never went through the terrible twos. Or the mom who has yet to see that child throw a full-blown tantrum or even make a potty error. But hey, trust us, those challenges are ahead. And the better we equip ourselves for them, the better moms we'll be.

You can't please everyone, Mom. You can't fix everyone and everything. Life is messy. You know it. We know it. One day our kids will know it. It's our job as moms to prepare them for this reality by modeling how to handle the messiness of life when people aren't happy all the time. If mama ain't happy, it's up to us to deal with it and up to our kids to let us. And if they aren't happy, it's up to us to let them learn to deal with the messiness too.

Why Saying No is Difficult

Real moms need to learn to say no to carrying someone else's load, or taking responsibility for someone else's responsibilities. Saying no is good because that protects us, but sometimes saying no feels bad. Knowing the reasons why it feels bad can help us move beyond those feelings and exercise our "no" muscles. Here are some reasons:

- Fear of hurting the other person's feelings
- Fear of abandonment and separateness
- A wish to be totally dependent on another
- Fear of someone else's anger
- Fear of punishment
- Fear of being shamed
- Fear of being seen as bad or selfish
- Fear of being unspiritual
- Fear of one's overly strict, critical conscience[6]

Real Mom Story

"Space for Me" by Susan Lawless

I never thought of myself as claustrophobic until my husband and I had children. Our house was plenty big enough for us to have our own space when it was just the two of us. And then they came.

Since then, my space is invaded every minute of every day. It seems there's nowhere that I can hide where my kids can't find me.

I thought that I could hide in the bathroom. One night after a very stressful day, I decided to take a nice hot bath. I lit a few candles, turned on some soothing music, and began to let the tension float away.

Then I saw them. Little fingers wiggling under the door. Next came the voices. "Mom, can I come in? I need to go potty."

"Use your bathroom," I replied in a strained tone.

"But I want to use your bathroom," whispered the voice on the other side of the door.

My closet became my next sanctuary. Crammed in with smelly shoes, an array of golf clubs, and a handful of chocolate candy, I smiled to myself, thinking that I had outsmarted them.

Then I heard a knock on the door. I was afraid to breathe. I hid behind a long trench coat as the door opened slowly. I heard a small voice whisper, "Mommy. I found you."

I'm not even alone in the car these days. I envy my husband who has thirty minutes each afternoon to be alone. He can listen to talk radio, drink his coffee, or just enjoy the silence.

Me? I'm riding in the car with two kids, one screaming to hear Shania while the other one wants the Backstreet Boys. I'm doing seventy down the interstate, threatening my kids with a paint stick, drinking a Diet Coke, changing the radio station, while still staying between the white lines. Now, that's talent.

When I go shopping, my kids are almost always in tow, which means when I need to go to the bathroom, everyone must go to the bathroom.

They stand outside the stall, asking, "Mom, aren't you finished yet? You really needed to go a lot! Are you pooping? Mom? Mom?" The woman in the next stall is snickering. I hope she doesn't have any toilet paper.

Don't get me wrong. I love my kids and I love to spend time with them. But I know I'll go crazy if they are my focus 24-7. I need a spot to call my own. A place for me to be by myself, a place where I can go to rejuvenate, and a place where I can put my things and no one will bother them . . . or me!

When I find this place, I'll let you know.[7]

Reality Check

1. Do you struggle with wanting your kids to like you? Does this desire ever get in the way of your disciplining them or saying no to them? How might your desire have slipped into an approval addiction? The need to be loved is certainly valid. If you can't lean on your kids to meet it, where else can you turn?

2. What kind of response might you expect if you stop taking responsibility for everyone's feelings and mood in your family? How can you prepare yourself and them for this adjustment in your role?

3. Think of a time you had to "contain" your child's feelings. Was it about sadness or anger or fear? What symptoms in your child can you watch for that signal the need for this skill?

4. Knowing God in a personal way doesn't necessarily prevent us from facing hard times but rather helps us handle our challenges in the midst of hard times. Can you give some examples of how you have learned that you can't fix everyone and everything, and that people aren't happy all the time? How has your relationship with God helped you through these moments?

5. Look at the list of reasons "Why Saying No Is Difficult" in the sidebar in this chapter. Which of those reasons might be your reasons? Where did that reason come from in your life? How could you deal with the difficulty you have in this area?

For Further Reading

Boundaries by Dr. Henry Cloud and Dr. John Townsend
Facing Codependence by Pia Melody
The Mom Factor by Dr. Henry Cloud and Dr. John Townsend
Women Who Try Too Hard by Kevin Leman

Real Moms . . .

- A real mom always loves her kids . . . she just doesn't always like them.

- A real mom puts her hands out to catch her child's unexpected vomit but misses most of it.

- A real mom knows she is doing something right when her child says, "You are the worst mother in the world!"

- A real mom will admit that there are seasons in which she has a favorite child.

Chapter 5

Lookin' Good Enough Mom

Real Moms Struggle with Their Looks

> I don't care how young or old, perfect or imperfect, confident or fearful, or mature or immature she is, every woman would like to be more beautiful than she is now.
>
> And most women don't think they are as beautiful as they really are.
>
> —Stormie Omartian

Myth: A good mom looks like a model, not like a mom.

Reality: A real mom struggles with her looks.

Summer. It's a great season for some moms. But for others . . . well, we just cringe at the thought of exposing so much of ourselves. Our arms. Our thighs. Our bodies.

There's the whole swimsuit thing. You're going to the beach for a vacation. This is wonderful. But you were pregnant last summer (oh, it was good to have an excuse to look the way you did . . .), and now there's no way out of swimsuit shopping.

Wonderful this is not. You dump the kids off at your mom's (there's no way you're doing this with them in tow), head to the mall, and flip through a few racks of suits that look like they'd barely cover your toddler's baby doll, much less your post-pregnancy body.

Sighing, you head for the fitting room, mulling over the meaning of that name in your mind. Like some magic "fitting fairy" will appear behind the shuttered door in that brightly lit and mirrored little room, automatically adjust your body to the swimsuit, and voila! A veritable bathing beauty you will be. Malibu Barbie in the flesh. Sure doesn't help that the *Sports Illustrated* swimsuit edition just arrived at the newsstand this week, painfully reminding you of what you're supposed to look like.

> **Who among us ever fit into an itsy-bitsy, teeny-weeny, yellow-polka-dot bikini – even before kids?**

Moms are supposed to look like models, not like moms. On the surface we know this statement is ridiculous. Who among us ever fit into an itsy-bitsy, teeny-weeny, yellow-polka-dot bikini—even before kids? The bodies of womanhood defy such accomplishments. We either have hips and boobs and therefore pop out all over, or we have neither, leaving the fabric flaccid, or we have some odd combination of one without the other, forcing us to sneak unmatched sizes in and out of the fitting room. There's that name again. Fitting room—what a joke! Fit-to-be-tied room is more like it.

So what's the deal? Why is this clearly insane myth about model-like appearances so compelling to grown women who are facing the much more important issues in life, like raising adults for the next generation? Because this myth is so pervasive. It starts way early in our culture. Preschoolers play with Barbie dolls, and prepubescents can't avoid the world of MTV, lusty song lyrics, and airbrushed photos of anorexic models that jump out of the television and magazines. And it's getting worse all the time.

In a study of more than three thousand middle-class fifth to eighth graders,

40 percent felt fat and/or wished they could lose weight,

30 percent had already dieted,

8 percent had fasted,

3 percent had pilfered parents' diet pills,

5 percent had forced themselves to vomit.[1]

And the problem gets worse. It's been said that one out of five college-aged women has an eating disorder.

Further, this myth is rooted in our roots, in the heritage we received from our mothers and the legacy they inherited from theirs. Females have struggled for centuries to define their worth by their appearance and their attractiveness to men. Our current culture elevates a concept called "lookism" as *the* judge of a woman's worth. Sociologist Mary Pipher, of *Reviving Ophelia* fame, defines lookism as evaluating others solely on the basis of one dimension—appearance. It's taking over the media, our schools, and our society. If you look a certain way—whatever's *in* right now—then you matter. If you don't, well, forget it. You're *out*. In case you

> **Females have struggled for centuries to define their worth by their appearance and their attractiveness to men.**

hadn't noticed (and of course you have!), thin is in. Miss America grew even thinner between 1979 and 1988. In 1992, her weight was 13 to 18 percent below the average weight for women.

Alas. We know this myth and the whole idea of lookism is nuts, but many of us still press on toward such impossible standards of appearance. We somehow think that if we're happy with how we look, then we'll be happy with who we are. Yet exactly the opposite is true.

To cope with this no-win scenario, we usually choose one of two tracks. On the one hand, we overcare. We throw ourselves into the myth, which triggers other illogical behaviors. We become addicted to shopping, always looking for the *exact* right, cool stuff (on sale, of course!) that fits just right and will make us feel like we look good. Or we start dieting and stop eating so we'll feel like we look good. Or we exercise more and more and more so that we'll feel fit and look good.

The other track? We go the opposite direction. We undercare. We simply give up on ourselves and the way we look. Convinced that we'll never measure up to the Buns of Steel and Abs of Adulation standards, we convince ourselves that we don't care. We resign ourselves to wearing sweats or oversized clothing, no-style hairdos, no makeup faces, and turn to Lays Classic chips or Oreo cookies for comfort. Or we give up on ourselves and throw our energy into the appearance of our children. We dress our daughters in darling outfits and push them toward gymnastic achievements that make us proud of their physical successes. We keep our sons cuted-up and spike their hair into trendy eye-catcher styles. If we can't meet the standard for lookism, we'll make sure our children do.

Overcare or undercare, either track leaves us at the mercy of this subtle, all-encompassing myth. In fact, they also ensure that such crazy thinking is successfully passed on to the next generation. We're doing our part!

Let's throw some reality checks into this myth once and for all. Ready? The average American woman weighs 144 pounds, and the average size for women today is a 14. (That's what Marilyn Monroe wore.) If Barbie Doll measurements were applied to women today, only one in 100,000 women would fit her mold.

(And she would most likely fall face forward due to the weight of her chest!) Moms are not created with equal bodies—model bodies, Barbie bodies, or *Sports Illustrated* swimsuit edition bodies. We are not airbrushed each day to remove any sign of acne, wrinkles, or drooping female parts. We are women who come in all shapes and sizes.

Real moms remove the mythical picture of the model body from their minds and from their investment of energy. They move away from the overcare and undercare reactions to a take-care posture of nurturing their appearance. They realize that their appearance reflects who they are. They know that they'll be more content with how they look if they are more content with who they are. In fact, many have come to believe that what makes a woman beautiful is knowing that she is loved not for what she looks like but for who she is.

Acceptance of several key issues helps real moms here. First, take care to accept your body changes. This starts in puberty. Remember getting your first bra? Ah, with a mixture of horror and hope, no doubt! Was everyone else getting one? Were you the first or the last to hit the mall for the perfect fit? Then there were the accompanying torments of acne, of getting your period (or not), of height and weight and oily hair and clothes selection and the battles that always started with, "But Mom—*everybody* is wearing this!"

Body changes continued in pregnancy with the awe and wonder of a life growing inside you and the utter terror of wondering if you'd ever see your own feet again. Your boobs were terrific! Your fingernails grew! And wasn't it grand to eat and eat and eat and eat and eat all that stuff because it was good for the baby?

Then came the great postpregnancy days. In *The Girlfriends' Guide to Pregnancy,* Vicki Iovine lists six legacies of pregnancy all too familiar to many moms:

1. Bigger feet
2. Smaller breasts
3. More skin
4. Darker nipples
5. Relaxed vagina
6. Lazy bladder[2]

Writer Anne Lamott humorously models the acceptance of postpregnancy body changes in her book *Traveling Mercies* by describing how her flabby thighs took on a persona of their own. She christened them "the Aunties," whom she took to the beach with her, even though they did embarrassing, unexpected things, like kept moving even after she had come to a complete halt.

Our bodies are going to change through all the stages and ages of life, and real moms know and accept this reality. That's right—next comes the changes that come with aging! (It ain't over yet!) And the attitudes with which we manage the postpregnant, after-kids changes will better equip us to maximize and accept the grandmother challenges. But that's another book.

> **And the attitudes with which we manage the post-pregnant, after-kids changes will better equip us to maximize and accept the grandmother challenges.**

Real moms also take care to accept their body types. For decades—maybe even centuries—experts have identified three or four main female body types. They are typically described as the Hourglass (curvy with an ample upper and lower body); the Spoon (bottom-heavy with heavier thighs and saddlebags); the Ruler (streamlined, with poor posture and weaker stomach muscles); and the Cone (top heavy with heavier arms, chest, and belly). No matter how much you diet or exercise, you can't change your basic body shape.

For a few moms, your God-given bodies fit you into some of the elements of lookism, and you will be evaluated well because of how you look. You happen to be tall and thinnish and boobish. For most of the others of us, we'll never meet the aspects of the media-model standard. So what? Join in with the group of women who unabashedly created a "Big Butts" video to firm up some of the excess they carry around. Good for them! When Oprah allowed cameras to journal her makeover process before a cover shoot for her magazine, catching her first without makeup and then showing her transformation, her mailbag overflowed with letters from women, thanking her for her honesty. We love to see each other in the raw, untouched-up, the way we are, real. Sure, it takes courage, but again, that's the kind of courage that builds confidence and translates into its own kind of beauty seen on the outside. That kind of courage and honesty yields freedom.

> **We love to see each other in the raw, untouched-up, the way we are, real.**

In her book *Love the Body You Have,* Marcia Germaine Hutchinson describes this kind of freedom: "We are so busy obsessing over what is wrong with us—whether it's our weight, misproportion, wrinkles, pimples, excess hair, or functional limitations—that we fail to develop our potential as human beings. If we could harness a tiny fraction of the energy and attention wasted in body hate and use it as fuel for creativity and self-development, just think how far we could travel toward life goals."[3]

And finally, real moms take care to accept their body's meaning in life. The body isn't just a body. It's a house for the soul. As God tells us in the Bible, the body is actually a temple where the Holy Spirit lives. In 1 Corinthians 6:19, Paul says, "Do you not know that your body is a temple of the Holy Spirit?" Wow. What does that mean? It means we're a whole lot more than a bunch of cells shaped into an Hourglass or a Cone or a Spoon. When God is in our lives, he lives within our souls, which is the reason that no care is not an option. That truth gives us plenty of reason to take good care of this "house for our souls," rather than to let ourselves go. That's reason enough to choose healthy habits and make the most of the bodies God has given us. As Mary Pipher puts it, "Accepting our bodies the way they are is the greatest gift we can give to ourselves." And, we'd add, the greatest gift of praise we can give back to God.

Here's the truth about appearance: moms aren't supposed to look like models. They're supposed to look like moms. We may still struggle with our looks, but we are *freed* when we remember that we are loved not for what we look like but for who we are. Yet we accept the responsibility to care for the body God has given us and to make the most of our appearance.

Real moms know that how we look doesn't make us content with who we are. Who we are makes us content with how we look. And because we're *real,* we *look good!*

■Real Mom Story■
"Beauty" by Lori Scott

When I was playing dolls with my three-year-old one afternoon, she unexpectedly set aside her Barbie and clasped my face in her hands.

"I love you, sweetie," I murmured as she scrutinized me.

"I love you too, Mom," she said, "but not your hair. Your hair is too short. It looks like a boy's hair. I don't like it."

I was stunned. Don't all children think their mom is beautiful? I found myself wishing we owned something like a Gap

How to Take Care of What You've Got

Being real means recognizing that how you look reflects who you are. Being real does not mean accepting your less-than-perfect self with a resignation that gives up. Take care of yourself. Make the most of what you've got. The world around you offers plenty of opportunities to do just that.

Take a risk. Get out of the same-old, same-old rut. Thumb through a women's magazine or catalog and check out the new styles and colors. Look for something that you could add to your wardrobe that would give you an updated look—a scarf, pair of shoes, a shirt or sweater in a new color. Step up to the makeup counter in a local department store and get a makeover. Paint your fingernails or toenails a bright new color, or try a new shade of highlights in your hair.

Get moving. You're not going to change your body type, but you can shape what you've got and feel more fit with a little exercise. Even if it means pushing the stroller around the neighborhood or up and down the mall, get moving. Weight training is one of the best shapers, so look around and see how many weighted objects you could use to flex your muscles. Keep a dictionary near the phone and exercise your biceps while talking on the phone. Many local gyms or fitness centers offer babysitting and plenty of motivation to get you going.

Eat right. You've heard this stuff a zillion times. Eat more fruits and vegetables. Cut back on sugar. Drink more water. Simple habits based on the simple idea that the kind of fuel you put into your body directly affects how you feel and look. So take a bottle of water with you in the car (your own sippee cup!) and sip away as you drive. Be proactive. Eat more sensible small snacks more often to fight the temptation of binge eating a whole bag of cookies in hunger desperation. Slowly savor your treats (like Oreos or chips) so that you appreciate their flavor and quality, rather than the quantity.

Toothed Barbie. I opened my mouth to respond, but she wasn't done.

"I don't like your nose, either. It's too big." Adding injury to insult, she honked my nose. Twice. Loudly.

"I see," I slowly replied, nursing my honker. "Is there anything else you don't like?"

She studied me carefully, finally declaring, "I don't like your chin. It has a funny hole in it."

"It's called a dimple," I said weakly, feeling like a warthog in jeans. I had always liked my dimple.

"But I like your eyes!" she exclaimed brightly. I perked up noticeably. "They're beautiful and blue, just like mine. They sparkle like sand fires." ("Sand fires" is preschool for "sapphires.") She batted her eyelashes at me dramatically. I mimicked her, giving her a butterfly kiss to boot.

"You know," I said, finally collecting my wits after these earth-shattering revelations, "you may not like my hair or my nose or my chin, but God made them just that way for a reason." Using my scariest voice I growled, "A big nose is better to smell you with, my dear." I snuffled at her. "A dimpled chin is better to tickle you with, my dear," I snapped, tickling her tummy. "And the hair . . . well, I'm not quite sure what to do about that, but Daddy likes it this way."

She was squealing with delight by the time I finished my antics. I concluded with, "I don't think I'll change a thing about me."

"Why would you want to change, Mommy?" she asked, pulling me into a fierce hug. "You're the most beautiful mommy in the whole world!"

Myths about Me

Reality Check

1. Hal Boyle writes, "Your body is far more intricate than the federal highway system. Inside you are some 100,000 miles of nerve fibers along which messages zip at speeds of 300 miles per hour." How does this quote help you respect your body?

2. "How you look reflects who you are." What does this statement mean to you? Is who you are on the inside reflected in how you look on the outside? Explain.

3. What area of your body do you have the hardest time "loving"? How can you help yourself change this response?

4. How can you "maximize" your appearance?

5. The Bible tells us that our bodies are temples of the Holy Spirit. How do you live out that truth?

For Further Reading

Then God Created Woman by Deborah Newman
Food and Love by Gary Smalley
Mom, I Feel Fat by Sharon Hersh
Reviving Ophelia by Mary Pipher

Real Moms . . .

- A real mom sometimes wears makeup, and when she does, her kids say, "Wow! Mom, you look different!"

- A real mom counts chasing a toddler around the house as exercise.

- A real mom vows (before children) that she will still have buns of steel at age thirty. But at age thirty (after children), she realizes that the only buns of steel she has come from sitting on cold, hard steel bleachers, watching small figures on a soccer field.

- A real mom considers her bathrobe a fashion accessory.

Chapter 6

Viagra Mom

Real Moms Aren't Always in the Mood for Sex

> The modern notion that sex is what gives meaning to the rest of the relationship has it backward. It is the sharing of the experience of life together as husband and wife that makes sex more meaningful.
> —Kenneth Chafin

Myth: A good mom loves sex and has it all the time.

Reality: A real mom isn't always in the mood for sex.

You've probably seen an ad like this on television. The camera closes in on a man's face, freezing a sincere expression. He looks virile, but as the words unfold, you find something is wrong in his life, something that is also affecting the life of his loved one. Yet because of a tiny blue pill, he has become a poster child for hope. His life has been transformed by . . . Viagra!

The first ads featured Bob Dole. An older man. A man who ran for president. But subsequent ads started featuring younger and younger men. All with similar stories. When the Bob Dole ads started running, the moms of young children thought, "Good for you, Old Guy! Keep at it!" When the ads started featuring younger men, moms winced. "You've got to be kidding! A pill my husband can take so he'll be Mr. Eveready? Geez, who needs that? I'm the one who needs a pill!"

The myth about moms loving sex bombards us from all sides. From the second we hit the checkout line at the market, we see the headlines touting "You Too Can Have Multiple Orgasms!" or "Women, Make Your Fantasy Life Come True!" It's tough enough to keep little fingers away from Skittles in the checkout line. Now we also have to deal with the emotional pressure of judging how well we measure up to these expectations. Should we be performing sex-goddess acts while also nursing, bathing, or feeding a preschooler? Who writes this stuff? And as for a fantasy life? That's a half an hour alone with a Diet Coke and a bowl of popcorn that we don't have to share with *anyone!*

But it's not just the hype of having *fabulous* sex that gets us down. It's the expectation of being available for sex 24-7. Media images make marriage with young children out to be one giant romp of making more young children. We live with the mantra, "Moms love sex and are ready for it all the time." Implied meaning? You're a blah-boring wimp-wife if you don't crave sex and spontaneously seek little quickies in daring places or odd moments of the day or night. Did you see the Chevy Chase family comedy called *Vegas Vacation,* in which the cutesy wife eagerly meets her husband in the tiny airplane lavatory for a quickie behind those flimsy folding doors while their children sit safely strapped into their seats a few feet away? Again, who needs that?

> **Media images make marriage with young children out to be one giant romp of making more young children.**

These nagging expectations about our sexual desires assault us when we wake up in the morning, and tangle us up as we fall back on our pillows at night. We must be doing something wrong. Who has the time? The energy? The interest? And we start to wonder, *What's wrong with me?* Am I weird? Am I normal?

One mom wrote to Dr. Ruth with this question, "Is it true that if someone is constantly eating and craving a lot of chocolate and sweets, those can be a replacement for sex? Or is it just that the person likes a piece of chocolate now and then?"

Dr. Ruth normalizes such fears with her answer, "There is something in chocolate that might make you feel better . . . certainly there are people who have all the sex they want but also have a sweet tooth, and of course kids adore chocolate but are not sexually frustrated."[1]

Are all the other moms in the neighborhood panting to jump into bed with their husbands the second they arrive home at the end of a long day? And even if they want to, *really* want to on some evenings, what do they do with the kids?

Here's a reality check. Studies show that 80 percent of married couples report that their sex life has suffered since becoming parents.[2] Fifty-five percent of moms with kids at home say they have trouble finding the energy to make love.[3] One sex expert cites the lack of interest in sexual activity—not just talking about it but actually performing sex in marriage—is at an all-time low. She goes so far as to call this a national epidemic.[4]

Moms love sex and have it all the time. Ahem. Guess that little mantra we've memorized just might be another myth, right?

Okay, now let's talk truth. Sex changes when children come into a marriage. Duh. That seems so obvious, and yet we have to remind ourselves of this fact. And of the fact that we are *normal* if we don't have the same sexual appetite as we did before children! As the adage says, "Sex makes little children, and little children make little sex." All the studies reinforce this fact. Testimonies agree (when people tell the truth). So what does this reality mean? And what are we going to do about it?

Let's start with just understanding it. How do children change sex in marriage? In our book *Children Change a Marriage,* we describe how children change the meaning and opportunity for intimacy, when husband and wife take on the new responsibilities of mom and dad. Children change who we are and how we respond to life. They consume us with their needs and take our primary focus off each other. Their distracting presence requires us to be intentional about investing in each other, which requires time and energy we don't often have.

Here are some reasons children change sex in marriage:

1. Your heart gets filled up with your child. Children change your heart. They take over all your physical and emotional space. As one mom puts it, "Our baby was our only passion. Marriage was an afterthought."[5]

2. Your body is different. After carrying around that extra baby weight, an episiotomy, nursing, up-all-night feeding sessions, and hormonal adjustments, how can sex ever be the same? Body parts that, prior to children, were reserved solely for sexual expression are now utilized for the maintenance of birthing, feeding, and burping ... twenty-four–seven. How romantic is that? Who wants to be touched there anymore today?

3. You're exhausted. By the time you've got the little ones down for the night, it's lights out—and not for adult playtime.

4. You're distracted. Just when mom and dad are finally reaching the big moment, there comes a tug and small voice from the side of the bed in the darkness, "Daddy, can

I have a ride next?"[6] You only have to hear that true story once and it's tough to forget that you too might have an audience.

Enough. Obviously children change your sex life. This is *normal!* So what are you going to do about it? You have a couple of options. You can give up and just forget about sex. Keep putting it off. Assume it was a passing fancy of your youth. After all, it's a lot of trouble. So why not accept these lowered expectations and simply cross it off your list?

Accept that you are a sexual being. As the sister gynecological team Dr. Jennifer Berman and Dr. Laura Berman comment, "Sexuality is such a central part of who we are, emotionally and spiritually, and when that's shut off, it shuts off part of our spirit as well."[7] To fully enjoy the benefits of the marriage relationship, we just can't give up! Does that mean sex is all there is to marriage, or that it's even the most essential element? Of course not. But the experience of sex is vital to the fullness of what marriage was intended to be. One author puts it this way, "Sexual union expresses, reinforces, and reenacts the marital covenant itself." The beautiful Hebrew euphemism for marital sex, "to know," helps us grasp this unique level of intimacy.[8] We are sexual beings. It is normal to acknowledge and enjoy this fact, even if our experience of it is not now where we'd like it to be. We don't need to give up and forget about sex. We can choose a different option.

> **The experience of sex is vital to the fullness of what marriage was intended to be.**

Let's go back to the Viagra ads for a minute. No, really. Even the concept of Viagra can put us in the position of having to cope with yet more expectations and readiness from our husbands. Or it can symbolize the hope of change in the midst of what is not a perfect situation. Take Bob Dole, for example. Following prostate surgery, he faced the choice of giving up on his sexuality or giving himself the choice of change. Viagra helped him. He faced reality and chose to change. What can help us? What are our options or choices?

Real moms accept that sexual stuff is a challenge when kids are in the picture. They recognize that children change their sex life. They understand that liking some things better than sex is normal. But they also acknowledge that sex can be better. Viagra moms take advantage of all that is available to them to make their sex life the best it can be, even in the trying times of raising young children.

> **What is it we really want from sex?**

Take a deep breath now and get real in answering this question. What is it we really want from sex? When experts surveyed women, they found all kinds of wonderful answers on our list. We want closeness, both physical and emotional. We want time with our husband. We want time to talk. We want romance. We want to be able to say, "Not now." We want to be appreciated for more than sex. And we want to please our husbands.[9]

We moms are women too. We are multifaceted beings who want to play, to learn, to partner, to parent, to pray, and to experience our sexual desires with our husband. In order to love ourselves—truly love ourselves—we need to reclaim *all* aspects of who we are. We reclaim our childlike playfulness by running barefoot with abandon across a grassy meadow. We reclaim our selves as social beings by having coffee with a friend and experiencing the joy of a growing relationship. And we reclaim our sexuality and romantic desires by taking good care of ourselves, which often means taking time out for whatever rejuvenates or renews our tired souls.

Myths about Me

How to Increase Sexual Intimacy in Marriage

Take your own sexual temperature. Just as some women shiver at 65 degrees and others are still hot-flashing, we all have our own unique sexual appetite. What is normal for you in the area of sex? Take yourself off the media's hook of sexual delirium and focus instead on your own very real sexual personality and level of desire.

Be aware of the issues that cause sexual intimacy to diminish in your marriage relationship. Busy husbands and wives often struggle with time for making love. (Experts label some of these couples DINS—Dual Income, No Sex.) Depression, marital conflict, and the lack of private time keep us from sexual enjoyment. Medications and hormones can alter your sex drive, as can pain, which is often treatable. See your doctor. Ask direct questions.

Talk together. The lines of communication about personal issues grind to a halt when little children consume your time and energy. Talk together, using real words, about your expectations or your desires. Ask each other what matters most. One couple that did this found that both wanted predictable times set aside for intimacy. They would figure, for instance, that Wednesday night would be their time together that week, and then, starting early in the day (or even the day before), they played a game called "Let the foreplay begin!" The game increased their tenderness toward each other for days.

Create an environment for sex in your marriage. Simple actions can lead to deeper levels of intimacy, like reclaiming your bedroom for privacy, using aromatic candles and music to enhance the mood, taking a bath or shower together (which even saves time and water!), declaring regular date nights, giving tender touches or massages with special scented lotions, writing love notes via e-mail, or simply taking time out to pamper yourself. These little ideas can help you and your husband think about sex and all that leads up to it.

Taking time out for ourselves? Every time we read such words, the silent cry is heard loud and clear: *But that's selfish! And who has time to take time out?*

As we've said before, taking time out for yourself is not self-ish. It's a matter of simple mathematics. You have to refuel an empty tank. You can't take out of the bank what you haven't put in the bank. You can't give to others when you yourself are empty. You have to fill up your own tank in order to have something to draw upon at the end of a twelve-hour day. Something to give your marriage because that matters. Taking time out for yourself whets your sexual appetite. When you are loving in this way toward yourself, you will feel lovable by others.

In the erotic writing of the Song of Songs in the Bible, we find this truth expressed, "This is my lover, this my friend" (Song of Songs 5:16). Before we got married, we chose our husbands because we hoped to have both elements of lover and friend in them. They chose us for the same reason. And a truly satisfying marriage makes room for both.

Real moms debunk the myth that moms love sex and have it all the time. They know that children change a marriage, and when they like some things better than sex (like sleep or time alone or chocolate), they know they're still normal. But they also know that sex can be better, and they care about how to make sex better.

■■■■■■ Real Mom Story ■■■■■■
"Light My Fire" by Lisa Moffitt

Once you have children, something happens to the romance. When it comes to the term "romantic parents," you have to work a little to make that happen. Even though romantic moments are few and far between at our house, Bill and I do work at being romantic parents.

For instance, one night not too long ago both of us had the same plan forming in our minds. We worked diligently to get the children to bed early. We did the bathroom check. We carried a glass of water to their room so they would not have to ask for one later.

When the coast was clear, we bolted upstairs to our bedroom. As Bill put on some romantic music, I lit a few candles. The atmosphere was just right.

We started dancing to the music and kissing a little. Bill decided to get a little more comfortable, so he threw his T-shirt off. We then continued to kiss and dance around our bedroom floor.

A few minutes passed and I thought I smelled smoke. I asked Bill if he smelled it and he replied rather hoarsely, "It's just me, baby." Silly me accepted that answer, and we continued to dance and kiss.

A few more minutes passed and I definitely smelled smoke. I opened my eyes and looked around. There was a fire on our night-stand. Bill had thrown his shirt on top of the burning candles.

Both of us scrambled to get the burning T-shirt out of the house. Talk about killing a romantic mood! I later told Bill that listening to the Elvis Presley song "Hunka Hunka Burning Love" will never be the same.

I know "romantic parents" is not the only oxymoron in a marriage, but looking at the alternative oxymorons, like spending a "small fortune" on a "civilized divorce," working at being romantic parents sounds like a great investment.[10]

Reality Check

1. What is your favorite thing about sexual intimacy with your husband? How can you build on this to improve your overall relationship?

2. In what area do you most fear you are not normal sexually? How can you find out if this area is a real problem and get help for yourself?

3. In what ways have children changed your intimacy? Have you talked with your husband about these changes? How and when could you discuss these changes with him?

4. Taking care of yourself increases your sexual appetite. How are you taking care of yourself? How could you improve?

5. Song of Songs in the Bible talks about "my lover, my friend." How do you invest in your husband as your friend? As your lover? How is your relationship growing in both of these areas?

For Further Reading

Children Change a Marriage by Elisa Morgan and Carol Kuykendall
Intimate Issues by Linda Dillow and Lorraine Pintus
Secrets of Eve by Archibald D. Hart, Catherine Hart Weber, and
    Debra L. Taylor
Sacred Marriage by Gary Thomas

Real Moms . . .

- A real mom thinks that occasionally the television makes a *wonderful* babysitter!
- A real mom gets a pedicure so she can use her toes in all new ways.
- A real mom does Kiegel exercises at stoplights.
- A real mom gets crazy once in a while.

2

Myths about Mothering

Chapter 7

Doin' My Best Mom

Real Moms Aren't Perfect and Don't Have Perfect Children

> The desire for perfection is the worst disease that ever afflicted the human mind.
> —Ralph Waldo Emerson

Myth: A good mom thinks there's a right way to mother and she must measure up.

Reality: A real mom isn't perfect but is doing her best.

Ever feel like you just don't measure up as a mom? Sure you do. Don't we all? One mom compares the challenge of trying to be a good mom to the challenge of dieting. Every day, she wakes up determined to be a good mom, but by midmorning, she's blown it! She's yelled at her kids, locked herself in the bathroom just to get away from them, and hollered "no!" at them twenty times. With dieting, she's at least able to make it through until lunchtime without digging into the bag of cookies or chips!

Sound familiar? Oh we try as moms, don't we? We check food labels for hyperactivity-inducing red dye. We pounce on backpacks in search of school newsletters, carefully transferring dates for activities to our calendars as we read. We make weekly trips to the library, where each child checks out three books. We read them out loud together (over and over), and then we make sure to return them by the due date stamped inside the covers. Pant. Gasp. Whew! We truly do try.

But there are so many moments when we feel like we don't measure up! After feeling proud of our patience with teaching the tedious task of tying shoelaces, we suddenly lose that same patience over a box of spilled Cheerios on the kitchen floor. Or we squeeze in a stop at the post office before lunch with tired and cranky kids (we knew we shouldn't), only to find a mile-long line of grouchy, kid-unfriendly adults who don't show any understanding for the trials of motherhood. Under their watchful, judging eyes, we let our little ones dump out the entire contents of our purse, just to keep them from playing peek-a-boo between our legs (or anyone else's legs). Of course we end up evaluating our mothering as *way* terrible.

We just don't measure up to the standards of good mothering—at least not the twisted perfect version we tend to hold in our heads. Did you get that? *Perfect.* The whole concept of measuring up assumes that there is an agreed-upon standard, a perfect way to mother. When we measure ourselves by the standard of perfection, we're sure to be disappointed!

In our better moments we may stop to ask the obvious but easy-to-overlook question, Where did this myth about perfect mothering come from? Our own mothers? That famous, faceless "somebody says" how you should mother and how your kids should behave? The Hallmark card definitions of motherhood?

The minister who offers his annual Mother's Day sermon? Oooh, how about the Proverbs 31 Woman from the Bible? Yikes.

> **B.C. (Before Children), most of us formed in our minds certain pictures of perfect mom-dom which still linger today.**

Maybe Martha Stewart is partly to blame. She gives us those images of a perfectly decorated home with perfect throw pillows (with perfectly hand-embroidered messages) and perfectly appointed dinner tables where moms effortlessly serve perfect meals to their perfect families.

Maybe we're partly to blame. B.C. (Before Children), most of us formed in our minds certain pictures of perfect mom-dom which still linger today.

- I will *never* pick green things out of my child's nose with my fingers.
- I will *never* let my child eat in the car.
- I will *never* be late to pick up my child from school or serve him microwaved meals in a box for dinner or let him watch three videos in a row so I can talk on the phone with my girlfriend.
- I will *always* be patient and loving.
- I will *always* know what my child needs.
- I will *always* be in control.

Never, never, never . . . always, always, always.

No wonder we can't measure up. No wonder one mom wistfully remarked, "I was a better mom before I had children."

Perfectionism is the drive to reach an impossible, unattainable level in some area of life. When this myth about the one "right way" to mother grips us, the result is dangerous. We fall into the performance trap in which we feel we must meet certain standards in order to feel good about ourselves. So when we don't measure up, we turn our eyes on ourselves in judgment.

Lousy mom. Not good enough mom. Bad, bad, baaaaad mom. We feel discouraged, depressed, disqualified, and discombobulated. There's no way for us to win.

Not only does this myth tie us up, it ties up our children—and theirs and theirs and theirs—with its legacy. As one expert puts it, "Perfectionistic mothers tend to either go crazy or make their spouse, their kids, or their kids' spouses crazy."[1]

> **Perfectionism is the drive to reach an impossible, unattainable level in some area of life.**

If we focus on trying to be perfect moms, just what are we subtly teaching our kids about us, about life, and about God? Kids don't want or need perfect moms. They need real life lived out before them by a real life mom who tries her best but makes mistakes sometimes. She accepts that about herself and learns how to lean into another Source of help with her needs. Children need to learn from example how to get back up when they fall, how to fix a problem they created, how to apologize for a mistake or an accident, how to make amends, how to wait for forgiveness, how to use an eraser or push the delete button. If we were actually able to accomplish perfection, why would we, or our kids, need God?

Real moms know they'll never measure up to the impossible standards of perfection around them, and they accept that truth as okay.

> **if we were actually able to accomplish perfection, why would we, or our kids, need God?**

Okay? That's right—okay. How can we say that? Well, because this is the basic truth of the gospel. God is perfect. We are not. We can give ourselves to the process of getting better and better at mothering by doing our best on a daily basis. But we don't have to live under the weight of impossible expectations that we'll somehow be *perfect* as women, as humans, or as moms.

The Bible underlines how we actually give God a chance to work when we are imperfect. Paul stresses in 2 Corinthians 12:9 that God's power is made perfect in weakness. His ability shines through our inability.

This brings us to one last important point about not measuring up to the standards of perfect mothering. Real moms know that doing their best is good enough in mothering but that it is not an excuse to stop trying to do better. Or to stretch and grow. As we've said before, God wants us to use what he's given us and always to grow toward becoming the best we can be. As the saying goes, God loves us where we are but loves us too much to leave us there. Or as one mother said, "I do the best I can until I know better, and then I try to do better."

> **Real moms know that doing their best is good enough in mothering but that it is not an excuse to stop trying to do better.**

Real moms aren't perfect, nor are they expected to be. When they don't measure up, they can be forgiven. They're hu-moms—moms in process—who do their best. That discovery makes us real.

━━━ Real Mom Story ━━━

"A B-plus Mom" by Brenda Quinn

In a moment of frustration while changing Collin's diaper today, I wished I had a grade awaiting me at the end of the day. A grade for mothering. An A-minus, a B, or even a C would help settle the questions that follow me from day to day. We had gotten together earlier with some other moms and babies. Collin screamed in the car for the last half of the trip there, and then screamed for most of the drive home. He finally fell asleep and slept through a quick

Prescription for Perfectionists

Diagnosis

Are you a perfectionist? Here are some questions to help you determine whether you have perfectionist tendencies.

- Are you quicker to dwell on your failures than your successes?

- Do you believe that if something is worth doing, it's worth doing well?

- Do you have trouble determining the difference between what's important and what isn't?

- Do you fear the possibility of failure?

- Is getting a C-plus okay? Do you need to get A's?

- Does it bother you to put a stamp on an envelope crooked?

Prescription

- Realize that some things aren't worth the time or energy, or that they take away from other things that are higher priorities.

- Try setting a reasonable amount of time to accomplish a task, and then make yourself stick to your deadline.

- Give yourself permission to say what's important and to change how you spend yourself in your mothering.

- Lower your standards.

- Put a stamp on an envelope crooked!

stop at Target but woke up as soon as I turned off the car engine at home.

I *hate* it when he cries like that. "Why did I try this?" I wonder as I drive, already far from home and helpless to quiet him. Am I permanently damaging him, allowing these car time cry sessions? Should I stay home and avoid the car trauma altogether? We can't stay away from the car completely! Maybe some crying is inevitable, maybe even okay?

I'd give today a B-plus. Collin seems fine now, and all in all we had a nice day. I just wish I could shake the lingering questions. I have a hunch they come with the territory of motherhood.

Reality Check

1. What aspects of mothering are important or interesting to you? (Example: reading to my children, providing good meals, being involved in activities with them.)

2. What aspects of mothering are not important or interesting to you?

3. Read Proverbs 31. The whole chapter. What do you think of this woman? Now be honest. While parts of this chapter may inspire you to improve and grow, do certain references intimidate or discourage you? Why might this be? Bible commentators offer help in interpreting this passage. One suggestion is that we are to realize that becoming this kind of woman is not immediate but rather a life-long goal to reach for. Okay. Another interpretation holds that this is not really *one* woman doing all this but rather that she is symbolic, representing a collage of characteristics and skills which we might aspire to in our lifetimes. There. How might these interpretations motivate you to grow in the area of perfectionism?

4. Dr. Henry Cloud and Dr. John Townsend write, "Good enough moms assume they will make mistakes with their child, and they factor that in to their mothering."[2] How can you "factor" your mistakes in to your mothering? When you make a mistake with your child, what steps can you take to repair the wrong for yourself? For your child? For perspective, look at 1 John 1:9. What does this passage say about how God views your mistakes? Now compare this truth with Psalm 103:12.

5. In the report card of mothering, what grade do you give yourself? Do you want to be an A-plus mother? What does being a good-enough mom mean to you? How can you be a good-enough mom?

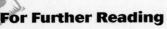

For Further Reading

Why Do I Put So Much Pressure on Myself? by Kathy Collard Miller
The Pressure's Off by Larry Crabb
Breaking Free by Beth Moore

Real Moms . . .

- A real mom watches Martha Stewart; that's all—she just watches her.

- A real mom shoves all the dirty dishes in the oven when an unexpected friend arrives.

- A real mom sometimes feeds her kids cookies for breakfast.

- A real mom doesn't take as many pictures the second or third time around. And when she does take pictures, she forgets to develop them for months instead of days.

- A real mom likes to drink orange juice out of the carton when the kids aren't looking because it saves time from getting a glass, and there's no clean up either.

- A real mom makes mistakes on a daily basis but keeps on chugging along, trying to get better.

Chapter 8

Mommy Wars Mom

Real Moms Like Their Way Best

> Seeing others around us differing from us, we conclude that these differences are ... manifestations of madness, badness, stupidity, or sickness....
>
> Our job ... would seem to be to correct these flaws.
> —David Keirsey

Myth: A good mom believes her way is the right way.

Reality: A real mom likes her way best.

The situation starts out innocently enough. A simple, mom-to-mom conversation about the everyday details of life.

"I can't believe Brandon will be going off to kindergarten this fall! I'm sooo excited!"

"Hmm. Well, we've decided to home-school Jessica. She'll do so much better in a more controlled environment where we know for sure what she is being taught. Besides, I'm really looking forward to doing this school thing all over again."

Differences. Natural. Normal. After all, people are different and we're going to parent differently. What's that to us? No big deal. Or is it?

Put yourself in Brandon's mom's mind as she drives home, minutes after this conversation.

"Good grief—home-school Jessica? She'll last about a month! That's for people who don't want their kids to ever grow up! They're so afraid of the big world out there that they'll keep their kids home until they're eighteen, and then they'll pick out their marriage partners for them. Sick. She is *wrong!*"

Ten seconds later, her thoughts turn a corner.

"What's *this* all about? What am I doing? I thought I was on the same page with my friend. I've always respected her. Why am I feeling so judgmental? Just because she's mothering differently than I am? Is it *wrong* to home-school Jessica? Will the child turn out okay? Is it just because she's choosing differently from me that I feel so defensive?

"In college we used to hang out at the coffee shop, talking about how we felt and what we believed. Then different was *good*. Different was *celebrated*. Why am I feeling threatened by differences today? What is motherhood doing to me? Why do other opinions seem *wrong* to me? I mean, my way *is* right—isn't it?"

Good questions. If only we would pause long enough to think—really think—about the answers. Is there only one way to mother well—*our* way? If another mother's way is different from ours, is she wrong? Or are we afraid that her choice might make our way wrong? Does everyone else have to be wrong for us to be right? Well, according to yet another motherhood myth, this is exactly what has to happen. And we can get surprisingly passionate in defending our way as the right way. Mothering can bring out the best in us, but it can also bring out the worst.

We stand in the checkout line and watch the mom whose child is whining for candy. When she gives in and says yes, we sigh and mutter, "She's ruining him." We exchange knowing looks with other moms when a friend's child throws a tantrum. "She needs to discipline that kid." We grimace at the working mom in our neighborhood who pulls into her driveway at dinnertime and unloads her child and all the stuff from day care. Or we roll our eyes at the stay-at-home mom dressed in sweats with no makeup.

> if another mother's way is different from ours, is she wrong? Or are we afraid that her choice might make our way wrong?

Whether the issue is public schooling, private schooling, or home schooling, working inside or outside the home, breast-feeding or bottle-feeding, styles of discipline or the number of hours allotted for TV, we moms find ourselves caught on the barbed wire of comparisons, a win-lose, right-wrong game. In the previous chapter, we talked about how we tend to judge ourselves as lacking because we don't measure *up*. In this chapter, the point is that we measure others against ourselves and judge *them* as lacking because they don't do it our way. We move from acknowledging the choices of others as different from ours to judging them as wrong.

How did we get in this spot? At the base of our choices is a nagging question: "What's *right?*" You've got to admit it, with no instruction booklet or operating manual accompanying the arrival of our first child, how are we supposed to know *for sure* how to raise this little darling right? We want so much to be good moms. In fact, we become passionate about everyone being good moms and the value of mothering for the ages. While this passion is good, what does it do to us?

There's no passion quite like this mothering passion. Mother love is a love of an intensity that surprises even us.

Carefully, we choose. Morning kindergarten over afternoon or no kindergarten. No sugar after dinner. Only an hour of TV each day. These choices seem to be working. We gain a kernel of confidence and make more choices. A play group. Trick or treating is allowed, but only to the houses of people we know. A part-time, work-at-home job which can be sandwiched into nap time and nighttime. An hour of videos is added to the hour of TV time. Gradually, we gain momentum with greater clarity and certainty.

> **Mother love is a love of an intensity that surprises even us.**

And then a neighbor announces she's found the "best" way to school through a private teaching group, expensive but worth it. Or she shares that any celebration of Halloween whatsoever is flirting with disaster. Or she hands you a book on the dangers of too much media. Instead of turning the accusing finger of judgment in on ourselves, we turn it outward to her. She's extremist, overboard, cocooning her child. She needs to get a life. She's nuts. No, sick. No, *wrong!*

From our separate corners of investment, we have the best intentions. Stay-at-home moms feel devalued by society and want to prove their significance. Working moms feel anxious and guilty about their situation and long to underline their real contribution to their families. The media doesn't help, as it pitches positions against each other, selling the view that we can't get along. As Anna Quindlen puts it, "It is a schism born of insecurities."[1]

Subtly, we conclude that if we are to maintain security in our mothering choices, everyone else who chooses differently must be wrong. In other words, we make others wrong in order to be right.

For several undeniable reasons, it's time to shatter this myth that there's a right way to mother. First, nobody knows the only right way. There isn't one. There's only the way that works for you and your family when your values and personality and unique situations are combined in your own life. What works for you may not work for someone else because moms are different. And children are different. And different doesn't mean wrong. It just means different. Sure, there are values or lifestyles you'll reject as inappropriate. That's obvious. But where we get in trouble is when we begin to judge others' best intentions and efforts as lacking or crazy or sick or wrong, just because they're not ours.

Second, we don't need to compete with each other when it comes to mothering. This isn't a contest. Granted, we live in a world that constantly judges and compares people, but God doesn't compare us. His love embraces differences, and so should we. Besides, there are great differences in culture and circumstances in the world of mothering. Of the approximately 14.3 million mothers of preschoolers in the United States alone, almost half are single moms and 56 percent are moms working outside the home. There are stay-at-home moms in suburbia, moms who speak English and moms who don't, teen moms, moms in inner cities, and moms living in rural areas. Approximately 2.6 million live below the poverty level. All different moms, trying to be the best moms they can be. Surely they will make different choices within their life circumstances. Are we to judge them for their choices?

> We don't need to compete with each other when it comes to mothering. This isn't a contest.

Most important, we need each other too much to fight. Being a parent is hard enough. We all are tired, anxious, and simply trying to do our best. It's time to embrace our common desire to be the best mothers we can be and to reach out to each other to help make that possible. We don't need to compete. We need to cooperate and encourage each other.

What is Your "Judgmentalism Quotient"?

Consider the following questions as you seek to better understand yourself as a parent.

- Do you have a high degree of sensitivity for children and for the ways they are nurtured and influenced? If so, do you usually bring your concern to God, or does it escape through judgmental words and attitudes toward other parents?

- Are you often insecure about the choices you make as a parent? If so, does your insecurity prompt judgmentalism toward other parents who have made different choices? Could you release your insecurity to God instead?

- Do you tend to believe in only one right way for most parenting issues? If so, you are likely doing a lot of judging. Have you asked God to help you better understand the differing choices he leads parents to make?

- Do you tend to be overly enthusiastic about your parenting successes? If so, have you asked God to make you more intentional in your sensitivity toward other parents as you share child-rearing stories?

- Do you feel drained due to the sacrifices you've made in your parenting decisions? If so, does your own need for affirmation cause you to judge the differing choices of other parents? Do you go to God for affirmation?[2]

And finally, the Bible tells us, "Do not judge . . . for in the same way you judge others, you will be judged" (Matt. 7:1–2). We often overlook the meaning because the words seem so harsh. In truth, these words tell us to be careful about judging—period. Only God is truly perfect, and therefore only he can judge fairly. When we judge others by our own imperfect, human standards, we can expect them to reciprocate, to turn the tables and judge us unfairly as well. We don't need to decide the rightness or wrongness of other mothers. Instead, as real moms, we accept ourselves— bloopers and all—and work to extend that same acceptance to other mothers. This is what Jesus means when he says, "Love your neighbor as yourself" (Mark 12:31).

In the beginning of this chapter, Brandon's mom asked herself a bunch of questions about why she felt so defensive. Why was she being so judgmental? By honestly asking and answering these questions for ourselves, we reach a new understanding.

Hey, let's be real. We all feel insecure at times in our mothering. We wonder whether we're doing it right. But instead of turning our doubts and insecurities into arrows of judgment aimed at all who mother differently, let's lay them down and tune our ears to what we can learn from the other mothers in our world.

◼◼◼◼◼◼◼◼ Real Mom Story ◼◼◼◼◼◼◼◼

"No More Mommy Wars" by Cynthia Sumner

I've been in skirmishes on both sides of the mommy wars— breast- and bottle-fed my babies, used cloth and disposable diapers. I earnestly tried, without success, to calm my fussy first child with a pacifier, but he would have none of it. The next two babies followed his lead. My jobs, apart from mothering, haven't required me to work outside the home. Instead I've enjoyed the best, and worst, of both worlds as a freelance writer working from home.

I relish being "right" about the mothering choices I make as much as the next woman. And I've taken my own mental potshots at moms who do things differently. But one experience really pointed out the ridiculousness of the mommy wars and how destructive and divisive they can be. At the time, a friend and I were publishing a newsletter for stay-at-home moms (SAMs). We were prepared for questions about why we were targeting SAMs as opposed to including working moms. (Answer: our experience was largely limited to being stay-at-homers ourselves.) But we were most surprised by a letter we received one day.

In it, a mother of four questioned—in the strongest possible terms—how we could possibly consider ourselves qualified to write on mothering issues since we had *only* two children apiece (that's four total). "You aren't a *real* mother until you have at least three children to care for," she wrote. Even when speaking to moms in our same demographic, we were not exempted from a surprise attack! I couldn't help but wonder how this woman treated her friends with only one child (if she had any). Did she give any validity to their comments?

After the birth of my third child, my business partner and I joked that at least now I could *legitimately* write about mothering issues. Even though I joked, I have to admit that I've never forgotten that letter, which still reminds me that my way is not the only way, and I need to accept the other moms who are different from me.

Reality Check

1. In what area of mothering have you felt defensive about your choices? Disciplining? Working? Schooling? Others? Why? Do you have a hard time accepting other moms' choices when they are different from yours? Why?

2. Is there someone you exclude from your life because you believe her different views are not "like-minded" or even "wrong"? How could you learn from her? How could you move toward including her in your life?

3. Have you ever seen this "different is wrong" attitude in your view of other children? (Not your own but maybe their friends?) This kind of judgment can subtly seep into our thinking. Take a minute to identify any ways in which you are judging other children as "not good for your children," "bad influences," or "weird, stupid, bizarre," etc. How might your attitude be affecting your children and what they are learning about acceptance and judgment?

4. Have you ever wondered whether God has favorites? You know, some people he likes better than others because they "do life" in a certain way? Read Luke 15:11–32, the story of the Prodigal Son, and see what you think. How does the way God loves all kinds of people motivate you to love all kinds of moms?

5. How can you truly free yourself to mother in the way you believe is truthful while allowing others to do the same?

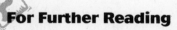

For Further Reading

The Mother Dance by Harriet Lerner

Great with Child by Debra Rienstra

What Every Mom Needs by Elisa Morgan and Carol Kuykendall

Mother in the Middle by Deborah Shaw Lewis and Charmaine Crouse Yoest

Real Moms . . .

- A real mom is truly and honestly excited about her child's accomplishments even though her friends' kids accomplished the same event *way* before!

- A real mom sometimes has to—or wants to—work outside the home.

- A real mom compares herself with her friends—and stops there.

- A real mom smiles at her little angels as she passes someone else's screaming brats in the grocery store—and knows she shouldn't.

Chapter 9

S.O.S. Mom

Real Moms Need Help

> This motherhood trip wasn't designed for lone rangers. It takes more than one woman against the world to raise a child in this increasingly complex and dangerous world. Even the pioneers sometimes circled the wagons. Women need one another.
>
> —Donna Partow

Myth: A good mom does motherhood on her own.

Reality: A real mom needs help.

Is this the way you think? If I ask for help, I'll be admitting that:

- I've made a bad choice to stay at home, because I obviously can't handle what I'm doing.
- I've made a bad choice to work outside the home, because I obviously can't handle what I'm doing.
- I obviously can't handle what I'm doing, so I'm probably not a good mom.

- I'm a weak, pathetic, incapable person.
- I'm exposing my weaknesses to the rest of the world, because I asked for help.

If any of this reasoning describes you, then this chapter is for you! This myth says that moms should do motherhood alone and that asking for help is bad. It's based on the belief that if you have to ask for help, then something is *wrong* with you. It means that you are not good enough. Or strong enough. Or capable of coping. It makes you appear helpless and threatens the perception of your success as a mom. Asking for help can put you in a position of owing others a payback. It opens you up to all sorts of risks in relationships. And this is bad!

How much sense does this make? Of course we can't and shouldn't do motherhood alone. We're really *healthy* only when we learn we have to ask for help. We need to overcome our crazy thinking here and become real moms. Consider your objections to using these sources of help available.

Kid Help. Okay, kind of an obvious one to start with. You need help, mainly with stuff that concerns your kids. They need to learn to help in order to develop basic life skills. A win-win, right? Oh, but here comes the but! They don't do it right! You have to do it over! They mess stuff up! Alas. And because of the but! you decide to handle it all, all by yourself, and they don't learn what they need to learn.

Ready for the next one?

Husband Help. Wow! That's another obvious one! You need help. He's around at least some of the time. He shares the same interest in the kids and the house and the marriage and the life you're building together. Major win-win! But! He does things differently than you do. He's rougher with the kids, less patient, doesn't know where the stuff in the dishwasher goes, always buys the wrong kind of laundry detergent at the grocery store, and lets the kids wear mismatched clothes to church. Or maybe he just gets irritated when you ask for help because you catch him in a moment when he'd rather be on the internet. Or taking a nap. And you'd rather keep the peace than get his help. So here comes that little but! And so once again you handle it all, all by yourself. But your husband not only misses out on a chance to figure out how to do stuff to help so that he can experience the benefit of contributing to the family. Your kids also miss out on experiencing what he might bring. Sounds more like a lose-lose situation.

Friend Help. Ah, now maybe this one is easier to receive. You need help. There's a friend available. You can ask for help . . . but! Then you'll owe her, and you've always said that when it comes to calories, money, or favors, it's absolutely awful to be in debt. Or if you let her take care of your kids, then you'll have to take care of her kids, and you *hate* taking care of kids—except your own, of course. If you let her run an errand for you, you'll be obligated to run one for her. How will you ever fit that in? If you share carpooling, you'll certainly end up on the short end since you live closest to the school, and you'll have to drive farther away to pick up the other kids. Oh, and here's the big one: if you owe her, she can call at any time to collect, and you won't have any control as to when that will be! No way! Your "but!" now means you do handle it all, all alone, and you get to feel lonely in the process.

Mentor Help. Hmm. Mentor help is help from someone who's just a bit further down the road than you are in mothering. The good thing is that there's usually no payback. How could you provide a payback to someone for information and insight that you don't really have yet? However, receiving mentor help does require taking on the stance of student. Becoming the learner. Becoming the humble one who doesn't know. And here comes the but! If we admit we don't know something in one area, then it might be assumed that we want or need unsolicited information in every area. The mentor might decide it's suddenly her job to tell us what to do in *all* areas of mothering, even those in which we aren't asking for help. Forget that! And so, forget the release from having to handle it all, all by yourself. Instead, welcome the doubts that come from not being able to check out your mothering theories with an experienced source.

It's pretty easy to "but!" ourselves right out of asking for help, isn't it? When we consider the sources of help available to us, we bump right into all these relational risks involved in using them.

> When we consider the sources of help available to us, we bump right into all these relational risks involved in using them.

Most of us carry around a whole backpack full of defenses that protect us from the hassles of relationships and, therefore, the experience of receiving the help those relationships can provide. Perhaps we experienced a childhood with an inconsistent or even hurtful parent who taught us to depend only on ourselves. Maybe we lost someone close to us early in life. Or maybe we found out the hard way that self-preservation can only be guaranteed through self-sufficiency. Whatever our history, we all have certain bruises and wounds from past relationships that influence our readiness to receive help today. Someone said that when we open ourselves up to others, we open ourselves not only to a lover's balm but also to a hater's bombs. Tough enough as stated, but we also lose control over where those bombs might hit!

A real mom lays aside her defenses against help because she knows that she can be the kind of mom she wants to be only if she both asks for and receives help. Moms were never meant to do motherhood alone. Sure, lots of moms parent without a husband. But that doesn't mean we were intended to mother alone.

> **Moms were never meant to do motherhood alone.**

God made moms for relationships, with himself and with others. The writer of Ecclesiastes puts it this way, "Two are better than one, because they have a good return for their work: If one falls down, his friend can help him up. But pity the man who falls and has no one to help him up" (4:9).

Asking for and receiving help grows us in our relationships. On the one hand, it helps us grow "up" as we develop the kind of intimacy that grows when two people share their vulnerabilities and both receive and give help to each other. Husbands like knowing they are needed. Friends feel valued when they can give help.

We grow "down" as we realize how very much we can learn from our children. "We need to help that man," our child tells us, tugging on our arm as we hurry around the homeless man who is struggling to push his grocery cart through the slushy snow at

> **Asking for and receiving help grows us in our relationships.**

the busy intersection. His shabby worldly possessions are falling out of the cart and the traffic light is about to change.

"Mommy," we hear our daughter as we're rummaging through the cupboard shelves, reaching for dust-covered cans of unwanted beans and fruit cocktail for our church's Christmas drive. "Mommy, I want to give this," she says, handing over her best doll.

These profound lessons from our tiny teachers give us a profound realization. Though we assume that God gives us these children so that we will grow and shape them into the people he created them to be, we soon realize, in these holy moments, that he also gives us these children to grow and shape us into the people he wants us to become. Learning to love more unconditionally. Learning to be awed by the wonder of his creation. As *Newsweek* columnist Anna Quindlen puts it, quite simply, "My children have been the making of me as a human being," and then she adds, as only a real mom can, "which does not mean they have not sometimes been an overwhelming and mind-boggling responsibility."[1]

> **Asking for and receiving help also lightens a mom's load.**

Asking for and receiving help also lightens a mom's load. Ever had the flu? Ever been stuck in traffic and unable to reach home before the school bus? Of course you have. And being able to reach out to say, "Can you help?" made the difference between being there for your child and not being there. Carpooling seems a hassle on your drive day but not on your day off. What a relief to experience the help of another!

Asking for and receiving help also provides hope. It's easy to lose it (hope, that is) when you're plugging away at all of life all alone. You are liable to start thinking that you're all

> **Asking for and receiving help also provides hope.**

there is and forget that there's more than just you in this mothering thing. Writer Anne Lamott remembers a time when a man from her church offered her some help after the birth of her son. "I sat on the couch while he worked, watching TV, feeling vaguely guilty and nursing Sam to sleep. But it made me feel sure of Christ again, of that kind of love. This, a man scrubbing a new mother's bathtub, is what Jesus means to me."[2]

And guess what else? *Asking for and receiving help helps others around us.* When we're able to use the four-letter word *help,* other mothers gain the courage to use it too. Then this crazy cycle of handling it all, all by ourselves, can stop, or at least pause.

Want to be a real mom? Take some risks. Give up the fear of appearing to be helpless, or worrying about owing people a

How Being Real Helps You Make Real Friends

When it comes to getting help, friends are pretty important. But developing friends takes time and a "friend"-ly attitude, especially the attitude of being real and vulnerable. Here are some tips about being real in order to develop real friendships.

Use selective sharing. Being real with someone doesn't necessarily mean opening up and dumping out all of your current thoughts, especially early in the development of your relationship. Selective sharing is best. Offer only appropriate information, which means that you share only what is yours to share. Avoid gossip or passing on rumors. Remember, being real is not permission to be a real rotten mom.

Acknowledge your "shadow." Some people refer to our hidden inner emotions as our "shadows," those feelings of anger or fear or woundedness. You can bring your shadow into the light by acknowledging these emotions. When appropriate, share them. Weakness can endear us to others, and we reduce the size of our shadows when we bring them into the light of sharing. When these emotions affect your developing friendship, share them with your friend.

Invest by owing. Friendships flourish on a unique kind of currency. Don't worry about owing or getting in debt when you help each other out. In fact, owing keeps friendships going. The more you give, the more you receive. Giving help is an investment in a friendship.

> The only way to have a friend is to be one.
> RALPH WALDO EMERSON

payback. Open yourself to the benefits of deepening the relationships with those around you who can offer help. We only pretend to protect ourselves through our many defenses! While those defenses may shield us from some potential discomfort, how much comfort they deny us!

One counselor prods us with these words, "We wrap ourselves in a protective coating to keep from getting hurt, but our lovely layers are ridiculously transparent, like Saran Wrap. That kind of protection only wraps you up tight and stops your pores from breathing. It does not keep anyone from seeing you; it only keeps them from reaching you."[3]

> **Asking for and receiving help helps others around us.**

Real moms *want* to be reached. They know they were never meant to do mothering alone. So they open themselves up to taking a risk to both ask for and receive the help they need.

■■■■■■ Real Mom Story ■■■■■■
"Seasoned with Love" by Renae Kramer

One snowy Saturday morning, I was trying to get breakfast on the table for my children. One was still in bed, one was having a bottle in the living room, two were fighting about nothing, and one was watching cartoons. As I called them to the table, it was obvious that my six-year-old was *not* in a very good mood. Now, it was Saturday, my *only* day to sleep in, yet I had gotten up early to make a nice family breakfast for my darling children, and my son was not going to ruin it with his bad mood! As he sat yelling at his two-year-old brother about sitting in the wrong chair, I was about to tell him that if he was going to be grumpy, he could just go to his room and stay there until his mood changed. Then I noticed my four-year-old get up from the table and walk into the kitchen. He took the spice container labeled "Love" off the counter. It has been a tradition in our home for the kids to pour some "Love" into our baking while they are helping me in the kitchen. Walking past me, he pulled me down and whispered in my ear, "Matthew is a little grumpy today, so it looks like he needs some extra love in his food this morning." He then walked into the dining room and poured the "Love" out on Matthew's food and over his head.

I was going to correct the situation by sending Matthew to his room. Conner saw the situation needed to be corrected by pouring out more love, even though his brother wasn't acting very lovable at the time. Praise God for teachable moments, especially when God uses our children to teach us a lesson.

Reality Check

1. Think back over all your friendships in life. Who were or are your real friends? What qualities make them fit in this category? In what ways have you learned to ask them for help? In what ways are you still holding back, and why?

2. Why don't you want your kids to help more? How can you ease yourself into being more open to what they can do? What do you have to let go of here?

3. Are you open to learning *from* your children? Becoming real moms means allowing ourselves to be childlike at times. Here's how you can grow a childlike heart. Can you add some other ideas for "growing down"?

   • Accept, admit, and embrace what you don't know.
   • Resist the urge to define yourself by performance and constant doing, doing, doing. Realize the value of your being.

Myths about Mothering

- Request help and applaud others who do the same.
- Open up, don't close up, to others.
- Model vulnerability by letting others see your needs and how you handle them.
- Ask questions.
- Use commas instead of periods.
- Admit your mistakes and apologize.
- Don't hold grudges.
- Find something awesome within your eyesight everyday.
- Get dirty.

4. In what ways is your husband open to helping? How can you encourage his help? What can you do to respond favorably so that he will help even more?

5. Name someone around you who could serve as your mentor. Remember, this doesn't have to be a perfect person, just someone a bit further down the road. How could you approach this person to ask for help? What kind of help would you like from a mentor?

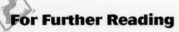

For Further Reading

Children Who Do Too Little by Pat Sprinkle
Make Room for Daddy by Elisa Morgan and Carol Kuykendall
No More Lone Ranger Moms by Donna Partow
The Friendships of Women by Dee Brestin
Patchwork Heart by Kim Moore and Pam Mellskog

Real Moms . . .

- A real mom needs other real moms.

- A real mom might act too tough and together to ever need help but would love someone pushy to insist!

- A real mom feeds her children lollipops (or just about anything) so she can complete a phone conversation.

- A real mom misses her old friends and having an uninterrupted conversation more than she misses fitting into her old jeans.

- A real mom asks her kids to pray for her when she's having a bad mommy day.

- A real mom realizes that while she is given the privilege of raising her kids, she is also given a window to the opportunity of raising herself.

- A real mom realizes that she learns as much from her children as her children learn from her.

Chapter 10

Busy Mom

Real Moms Have Too Much to Do

> I try to keep up. I really do. But sometimes I feel like I'm one step ahead of chaos.
> —Elizabeth Cody Newenhuyse

Myth: A good mom does it all, all right, and all right now.

Reality: A real mom has too much to do.

Perched on a platform high above the circus ring is a woman wearing a T-shirt with "M-O-M" on the front. She does a few stretches to warm up, and then places a unicycle on the high wire. Ever so carefully, one foot at a time, she positions her body atop the cycle. Though wobbling a bit, she checks the list crumpled up in her hand, and then reaches around for some of the stuff piled high on the platform: two backpacks, a diaper bag, a soccer ball, a plate of homemade brownies, a Daytimer, and a cell phone, to name a few. Finally she is ready and cautiously pushes herself away from the platform. Once on the wire, she begins pedaling her way across, inch by inch, balancing all the stuff and the unicycle while making several calls on the cell phone, eyes shifting between those objects and her goal, which is to reach the platform on the other side. She nearly loses her balance a couple of times but, at last, she makes it to her destination, tired and triumphant, and the audience responds with great approval. Ta-da! She made it through another day!

This is today's Busy Mom, a multitasked, ever-moving, energizer kind of woman who's learned to move past the myth that says good moms have to do it all—today. Right now. A real mom embraces the truth that moms have too much to do, but they can find balance without tumbling from the high wire of life. She's learned to sort through all the stuff and make some choices.

> **Busyness is inevitable. It's part of being a mom.**

Where do we get the "do it all" myth about busyness? The truth is, moms are busy. Mothering young children is a season in which demands are constant and resources are few and many responsibilities are not optional. So moms reach down into the very essence of their reserves and come up with their own creative combination of skills to meet a variety of needs. Great, huh? Well . . . sometimes. But that doesn't simply do away with the busyness. That's because busyness is inevitable. It's part of being a mom.

The tricky myth about busyness is the belief that moms should do it all, do it all right, and do it all right now. Just as we begin maneuvering our way across the high wire of life, having mastered the art of balancing our most obvious responsibilities, we then expect ourselves to also start spinning plates, juggling balls, and performing gymnastics as well. All at the same time. Perfectly. We add more and more stuff without subtracting any stuff, thus setting ourselves up for losing our balance and toppling over.

This is the mom who has chosen to stay at home but has added the responsibilities of a growing at-home business, so she packs her kids into the minivan to do errands and attend other at-home business parties several days a week, and leaves them at home with hubby or a babysitter three nights a week while she attends cropping or stamping parties, toy showings, or business meetings. Home economics has taken on a whole new meaning with the advent of all these at-home businesses.

This is also the mom who has chosen to fit kids into her career with a careful timetable of day care and work. Passionate to be involved in her child's schooling and determined not to let her work interfere, she devours every school newsletter and volunteers for every school activity to avoid any hint that her work jeopardizes her ability to do it all.

Then there are the moms who, whether or not they work outside the home, migrate from one Bible study to another. And the exercise junkies. And the shoppers, or the book group moms. Oh, and the craft women, armed with glitter and glue guns, who aim at anyone who threatens to take their time away from their creative outlets.

Busyness comes in all packages.

Now let's be clear:

1. *There's nothing wrong with being involved in this stuff!* Most of it is good stuff, and great moms everywhere participate in many activities and/or work responsibilities. They are still great moms.
2. *There's nothing wrong with at-home businesses!* The opportunity to work from home on one's own schedule is a huge benefit to moms of all ages who want to be present for their kids while augmenting their income. All the home

businesses mentioned previously offer solid work opportunities and quality products.

3. *There's nothing wrong with having a life!* We need outside
interests. In most cases, they make us better moms. They
help restore perspective and focus and meaning in our
lives and in our mothering moments.

4. *There's nothing wrong with some stress in life!* In fact, mental
health experts agree that "healthy stress" is necessary for a
meaningful life. If we didn't face some degree of stressful
demands in our days, we'd all become couch potatoes.
The reality is, life is busy. We face lots of tedious tasks in
mothering, and living a life that matters means living with
some element of stress, busyness, and investment.

What's wrong is what's beneath the myth or the reasons for
overcommitment. One is we can't say no. As women, we've
accepted the mantra that if there's a need, it's ours to meet. Because
meeting needs makes us feel loved, important, like we matter.
Meeting needs is a currency we understand and can control.

> We've accepted the mantra that if there's a need, it's ours to meet.

A friend is giving a party to sell the latest in cookware, so we slam down the box of
Hamburger Helper, mix it up, serve it up,
and leave. A neighbor needs help moving;
we go pack. Our kid's teacher calls for Friday treats; we bake
cookies. On the surface, no big deal—added responsibilities that
aren't even obvious to those around us. But when we add task
after task and commitment after commitment without subtracting any of the responsibilities we're already carrying, our legs
begin to stiffen and we begin to wobble as we continue to inch
the unicycle through this season of motherhood. Too much
weight to balance. Too much stuff. Overcommitment.

Another reason we struggle with overcommitment is a deep-down desire for value. Doing lots of stuff makes us feel like we're worth something. Accomplishment equals value. Admit it, when the most you produce in a day is a counter clear of dishes or making it to day care on time, you start to question your contribution to the planet. But when you create a scrapbook full of permanent memories, edged with patterned borders symbolizing the various holidays, you feel more valuable. Who wouldn't?

And then there's one more reason for overcommitment. We think we're supposed to. A good mom is committed to do it all, do it all right, and do it all right now. We want to be good moms. But such expectations are ridiculous and unrealistic. One mom comments, "Moms should never turn their backs on their little ones. They should be there always." (It's that *never* and *always* thing again.) That's tough when you have to earn a living, stop to fill the car with gas, shop around for the best bargains, and throw in a load of underwear and socks, all before you show up on time to take tickets at the spaghetti dinner fund-raiser at school. We can relate to the mom who concludes, "We try to squeeze Martha Stewart expectations into a McDonald's time frame."

> "We try to squeeze Martha Stewart expectations into a McDonald's time frame."

We can find some understandable motivations for living within such a stressed pattern of life. But yikes, there are unpleasant results as well. When we overcommit, we lose our balance. Just living with this tension takes its toll. We're constantly feeling tired and get angrier more quickly. We have shorter fuses. When we blow, we blow bigger and have more messes to clean up. We build up resentment in ourselves and in our family members, and our kids get butt-in-seat paralysis from living in the car. We forget how to have fun, which is bad for us and bad for our children.

When we overcommit, something deep inside of us slips out of focus, or as one mom describes it, our soul falls asleep. "Everything given *plus* little replenished *equals* desperately empty."[1]

Yuk. Not what we want, is it?

Busyness and balance are tough issues for mom. Truly, if we want to do even a decent job with our kids, busyness is inevitable. But the level of busyness differs, mom to mom. Some moms can handle more busyness and stress than other moms. They thrive best when juggling three balls and spinning two plates. Others prefer to carry only the necessary responsibilities during this season of life. Neither way is right or wrong, but a mom has to know how she's wired in order to accept and live within her capacity for busyness.

The key is to find balance in the busyness, and a real mom finds that balance by choosing what she'll be busy with. What matters most and what she can handle and who she is, with her unique characteristics. Did you get that? The key word is a verb. She *chooses*. And by *choosing,* she finds *balance* in the midst of the myth that moms should do it all, do it all right, and do it all right now. Here are some examples of choosing:

- We find balance when we choose between ourselves and others. No argument, mothering involves sacrifice, especially the mothering of young children. Our necessary tedious tasks that we do or delegate include keeping a house clean enough to survive, doing laundry, planning meals, and making ends meet financially, to name a few. We need to face the fact of some self-sacrifice and learn to live with it and do it. But we can't sacrifice without self-attention too. We can't do it all.

- We find balance when we choose between good and good enough. We need to set ourselves free from the temptation of overcommitting and trying to reach unattainable standards of perfection. We can't do it all right.

- We find balance when we choose between today and tomorrow. What can we do only today because it won't be there for us to do tomorrow? Mothering younger children requires different choices than mothering older children. We don't want to be so rushed to get to tomorrow that we miss the joy of journeying through today. We ask ourselves what is most important in this season of life because we can't do it all right now.

We're human. Elizabeth Cody Newenhuyse writes, "This is what we need to remember: God created us as limited human beings. We are not gods, endlessly self-sufficient, boundlessly talented. There is no sin in acknowledging we cannot do it all. And . . . there is a joyful freedom when we do assert our limitations."[2] Her words echo Paul's from Romans 12:3, "Do not think of yourself more highly than you ought, but rather think of yourself with sober judgment, in accordance with the measure of faith God has given you."

Real moms are busy moms who know that they get from one end of the high wire to the other each day by choosing what they carry. They find balance in spite of their busyness.

━━━━━━Real Mom Story━━━━━━
"Playtime" by Julie Perkins Cantrell

Welcome to my home. Please have a seat. Oh, sorry, you can't sit on the sofa. The cushions are all on the floor. Our little architects have arranged them to protect the sleeping princess until the handsome prince arrives. Of course, the rocking chair is probably not a

Simplify! Simplify! The Key to Finding Balance in Activities

Most moms are too busy. We know that, but in the midst of our busyness, we can find some balance by simplifying our lives. Here are some suggestions:

1. **Acknowledge that you want to make some changes.** Then decide that you are willing to be intentional about making those changes. This is the first and most important step.

2. **Take a time and activity inventory.** Look at your calendar and schedule. See what you or your children do regularly and ask yourself, Do I or does someone else in our family truly enjoy this? Prioritize the activities. What are your top three, the ones that are important and are making a difference in your life or theirs? Which are helping them grow? What are you doing that only you can do? What are you doing that someone else could do? Who can you delegate some or all of these last ones to?

3. **Cut!** Eliminate at least one or two of the activities at the bottom of your list, the ones that you are willing to cut to gain more "nothing" time for the family or more "just for me" time. Schedule at least one regular afternoon or evening a week for doing nothing at home. Protect that time wisely. Don't cut out all the "just for me" time either.

4. **Make time for fun.** Fun lightens your load, so lighten up and give yourself permission to have fun, even in the midst of doing other stuff. Dinner can wait. Christmas cards can arrive around New Year's Day. Weeds can grow in the garden for another day. The answering machine can catch the phone. Have fun in your own style, but don't miss out on the fun all around you.

5. **Check your traditions.** Have you outgrown some? Can you trade an old one for a new one? Are you having an annual Fourth of July party that depletes you and keeps you from doing other

important family activities? Do you go to the same place every Labor Day that has gotten to be more trouble than it is worth? Are you part of a lunch bunch that has outgrown its original purpose? Check your traditions.

6. **Choose wisely.** Never say yes right away to a request that demands an ongoing commitment. Take some time to think about the request and what it will mean in your schedule. Don't add a new activity without taking out an old one. Pick the best. Say no to the rest.

7. **Review activities every season.** Now that you have cleaned your calendar, commit to reviewing your activities regularly. Just as you clean your closet, your calendar needs a regular review.

safe option either. The fire-breathing dragon is often seen peeking from behind that chair. If you hear her roar, don't be alarmed. She won't attack you, as long as you carry your magic sword.

Perhaps we would be safer if we just avoid the living room altogether. However, the bedrooms have been converted into secret caves where the wild bears are hibernating. If we accidentally step on a twig while hiking through the deep-forested stairway, we could wake them. Besides, the hallway has been booby-trapped to catch the aliens that landed in the back yard last week. They've been rumored to sneak around the house after dark, but we haven't yet caught one. The bathroom should be safe, if you're willing to wrestle the man-eating shark that lives in the bathtub.

How about the kitchen? Please watch your step around the assortment of pots, pans, and serving utensils positioned across the tile floor. Our budding musicians will begin band practice in about ten minutes. Stick around. You'll be amazed at how well they can play percussion in tune to "Frère Jacques." I'm sorry I haven't swept the floor since breakfast. Adam likes to eat the pancakes off the floor, so I would hate to disappoint him. By the way, have you seen a remote control? The last time it disappeared, we found it hidden in my hiking boot.

Oh, you just wanted to drop off a magazine? Thanks! Just put it on the microwave, next to the purple wand and the broken magnifying glass. I'd do it for you, but I can't turn my back right now. The dragon has been known to attack the prince when she thinks I'm not looking. Watch out for the ant farm! Ah, well, there's plenty of pancakes for them to eat down there.

You have to go now? Well, come back soon. Just be sure to bring a sword, some earplugs, and a bottle of ant spray.

Reality Check

1. Some things are worth *not* doing well. Vacuuming before company comes over. Washing your hair before going skiing when it'll be under a hat all day. What are some others? Name three that are worth not doing well in your life right now, and how will you do them "less than well"?

2. What activity or task could you subtract so that you can add one for *you* that would give you a feeling of replenishment? What is the activity you will add?

3. Choose what to just say no to in your days. Fill in the blank: "I'll just say no to _____."

4. What are your barriers to finding fun in the midst of mothering? How can you give yourself permission to play more often?

5. Too much of any good thing can just plain be too much. What are some of the good things in your days that might be moving into the category of too much of a good thing? What steps can you take to cut them back?

Myths about Mothering

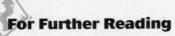
For Further Reading

Women Who Do Too Much by Pat Sprinkle
Growing Weary Doing Good by Karla Worley
Calm in My Chaos by Elizabeth K. Corcoran
Having a Mary Heart in a Martha World by Joanna Weaver
The Overload Syndrome by Richard A. Swenson

Real Moms . . .

- A real mom doesn't vacuum everyday.

- A real mom doesn't always make her bed.

- A real mom uses real plates when entertaining guests. But lots of times the family gets paper plates.

- A real mom gets under the table when her kids want to play "fort," even though the sink is filled with dirty dishes.

- A real mom hardly ever gets *all* the laundry folded and put away. She just grabs wrinkled shirts from the pile.

- A real mom knows how to say no.

- A real mom knows the true meaning of "eat and run."

Chapter 11

Worry-Some Mom

Real Moms Worry about Their Kids

> Can it be that parents are sentenced to a lifetime of worry? Is concern for one another handed down like a torch to blaze the trail of human frailties and the fears of the unknown? Is concern a curse? Or is it a virtue that elevates us to the highest form of life?
>
> —Erma Bombeck

Myth: A good mom protects her kids from all the bad stuff in life.

Reality: A real mom worries that bad stuff will happen to her kids.

She waited and waited and waited for a baby of her own. All the other elephants had received theirs but alas, she seemed to be overlooked. Finally, the stork swooped down upon the circus train and delivered a baby elephant to this hopeful mother. Amid the long-awaited praise from her friends, she lovingly caressed her new baby with her trunk, welcoming him into her heart and receiving every compliment into her soul. At last, the adulation she longed for! Jumbo Junior, she'd call him, after his father.

But suddenly, the baby elephant sneezed, unleashing his ears—a full three to four sizes larger than average. The other elephants guffawed. Jumbo? This baby was no Jumbo! Assuredly his name would have to be changed to match his looks. Dumbo! This baby elephant was Dumbo! Their compliments suddenly turned to ugly insults.

At this, the new mother snapped her trunk and slammed the gate shut on her noisy visitors. Her precious baby would not be ridiculed! Not if she had anything to say about it!

Days later, the circus train stopped and set up in a new city, where, as always, children arrived to gawk and explore. The baby elephant was quite an attraction, which was fine with mom, until things got out of hand. Tripping on his oversized ears, baby Dumbo drew giggles and sneers, taunts and pokes. That was too much for his passionately protective mother, who rushed to attack her baby's opponents. In the chaotic scene that followed, the ringmaster carried Dumbo away and carted his dear mother to the "jail" car, labeled with a sign that read "Mad Elephant."

In this classic Disney children's movie, we find a universal adult message about mothers. We can't really blame Mrs. Jumbo, can we? After all, the other elephants were making fun of her baby! Any one of us would probably have responded in the same way. We can overlook unkind remarks intended for us or even for another grown-up loved one, but such unkindness directed at our child? No way! When it comes to protecting our kids, we become fierce and attack, just like mother bears or mother lions or mother elephants. (Animals everywhere and mothers of all cultures display this same instinctive response when it comes to protecting their young.)

Good moms protect their children from the bad stuff in life; bad moms don't. This myth is tricky because it starts out as truth and then moves to impossibility and even to harm.

Huh? But we *love* our children! How can protecting them be harmful? Well, love that starts out as protective in the mother-child relationship needs to change with each developmental season. We moms have to learn to transition from expressing our love as protection with infants and babies to expressing it in other ways as our children mature. If not? We'll be trapped in a world of worry and our kids will be trapped in our protective shield, never able to grow up.

> **We moms have to learn to transition from expressing our love as protection with infants and babies to expressing it in other ways as our children mature.**

This can be challenging. Every mother wants to protect her kid from the bullies and pain and bad stuff of this world. She forgot her homework? Oh, just run it up to school. It's only a few blocks and then the child won't get points off. Good grades make us all feel good—kid and mom, huh? He struck out at bat . . . again? Rats. And we prayed so hard! Oh well, shoot him full of praise. Criticize the pitcher and the umpire. Make him forget his errors. Tell him how great he is and next time he'll knock it out of the park! That will make us all feel good.

We swallow the myth that good moms protect their kids from all the bad stuff, and we often end up overprotecting. We swoop down to intercede before he experiences discouragement. Helicopter Mom. We cuddle her up in an embrace with cocoa and cookies to distract her from the meanness of a girlfriend. Fix It Mom. We punch our videos into the VCR at home, forbid rap music on our car radio and exorcise all sugar from our cupboards. Cocoon Mom. Rescue Mom. Safety Net Mom. Our job is to keep our kids safe from all the world's stuff out there!

Or is it? Is that really a mother's job, keeping her kids safe? Protecting them from the bad stuff in life? Is this really even possible? For example, who can prevent strep throat? Okay, maybe you can try to protect a child from germs by keeping him home from school and church and rejecting his request for playmates. . . . Naw, you really can't protect him from germs, and is our job as moms to protect our children or is it to prepare them?

> **When our children are very, very young, we prepare them by protecting them. But as our children grow, we protect them by preparing them for real life.**

What's a real mom to do? Learn the difference between protecting and preparing and accept the reality of *some* worry in the process. Here's the truth: when our children are very, very young, we prepare them by protecting them. If we didn't hold up their heads to feed, they'd choke. If we didn't take their hands while crossing the street, they'd be hit by a car. If we didn't train them not to touch a hot stove . . . you get the point. But as our children grow, we protect them by preparing them for real life. We teach them how to handle the bad stuff that comes, so they can recognize it and handle it themselves later on. Real moms allow their children to realize that they're not good at *everything,* that sometimes they will strike out and lose the game and that they might not always make A's and B's. In short, real moms do their children the favor of exposing them to the bad stuff in the world, knowing that learning to cope with the bad stuff will help prepare them for life, in which bad stuff happens.

Sounds harsh and hard. It is. But it's worth it, because when we remember this goal of our mothering, we realize this is the way to become better mothers. We can't change the world for our children, but perhaps we can change our children for the world. We can't change someone else's unkind child to make him be kinder to our child, but perhaps we can change our child to learn to live with unkind people in the world.

Real moms understand this realistic responsibility. So naturally, real moms worry some. They worry some because they know that *some* bad stuff will happen to their kids, but they keep their eyes on who their child is becoming as he or she learns to cope with life's bad stuff.

How does this work?

The first step is the toughest. Let go and trust God with your child. Oh, right. But really, this is where preparation, rather than protection, begins. Think about it this way. As a mom, you want to raise a healthy, independent, well-adjusted child who handles life on his or her own. Right? To prepare them for whatever they might face as young, middle, and older adults, you have the chance to help them practice handling life as a child. And they can't learn to handle life themselves when you're handling it all for them.

> We can't change the world for our children, but perhaps we can change our children for the world.

While your child is a baby, you carry her about. It's easiest for both of you. She likes it. You get where you need to go. But as she ages, you have to put your child down, let her learn to walk, to run, to look both ways and cross streets alone, to drive, to date, to explore and study. She can't do that if you continue to carry her, can she? What works for the child in early childhood does not work for her in later childhood. Inappropriate protection or cocooning becomes more about our need to be in control than the need of our children to grow up.

We need to understand here that we're not letting go or laying down our child to just nobody at all. This vital step of release is one of placing her into God's hands. Long ago, Martin Luther observed, "I have held many things in my hands and have lost them all; but that which I have committed to God, that I still possess." In Proverbs 3:5–6 we're advised similarly: "Trust in the LORD with all your heart and lean not on your own understanding; in all your ways acknowledge him, and he will make your paths straight." Notice the word *lean*. Just as we're not to lean on ourselves and our understanding, as moms we want to teach our children not to lean on us ultimately but rather to lean on God.

No doubt, this is the hardest aspect of mothering for so many of us. That's why we're saying that real moms are Worry-Some Moms. Even when we choose trust, we'll still struggle. What worked only a few years ago just doesn't work as our children grow up. We are agonized by the challenge of holding back our arms from an "uppie" moment that really doesn't require our picking up and protecting our child but rather asks us to *prepare* that child. Understanding the process of maturity helps, how it happens in the lives of all of us as humans. See, we don't learn all that much in the fat times of life. Rather, it's in the skinny times when there's not enough or there are no answers. It's in times of trial that we really grow. "God, it has been said, does not comfort us to make us comfortable, but to make us comforters. Lighthouses are built by ex-drowning sailors. Roads are widened by mangled motorists. Where nobody suffers, nobody cares."[1]

Surely this is what Paul meant in Romans 5:3–5 when he wrote, "We also rejoice in our sufferings, because we know that suffering produces perseverance; perseverance, character; and character, hope. And hope does not disappoint us." We grow in all these aspects when we learn to deal with the bad stuff of life.

Understanding this maturing process helps us and helps us help our kids, but help increases when we move past just understanding it to modeling it in our actions day in and day out. Allow for mistakes. Expect failure. Welcome both as teachable moments and opportunities to teach critical-thinking skills. Show your kids where you turn when you face the illness of a loved one, the loss of a job, when a rude or crude person crosses your path, or a television commercial represents something you reject. Show them where you turn when life is hard.

Ruth Bell Graham, wife of evangelist Billy, models this stance for mothers in her prayer, "Hebrews 1:3":

> Listen, Lord,
> A mother's praying
> Low and quiet:
> Listen, please.
> Listen what her tears
> Are saying,
> See her heart
> Upon its knees;
> Lift the load
> From her bowed shoulders
> Till she sees
> And understands,
> You, Who hold
> The worlds together,
> Hold her problems
> In Your hands.[2]

Real moms move from protecting their children in life to preparing their children for life. They expect the bad stuff to come, and they use it to prepare their kids to handle those challenges on their own. Real moms expect to worry some. But they also look past their worries to see the bigger picture of what God can do with the bad stuff of life in the lives of their children.

How to Handle the Worry Habit

While real moms accept that some worry is inevitable, they know that constant worrying burdens us with a weight we shouldn't carry. "When worry gets a grip on us, we can't be clear information seekers, or clear decision makers, or clear anything. Instead, we *over* react or *under* react . . . or we yo-yo back and forth between the two. Neither helps and both can make the situation worse."[3] So why do we worry? Because it's a normal response to the responsibility of mothering. It's part of our job description. It goes with the territory. Some worrying is good; it keeps us on our toes as moms. So let's look at ways to handle the worry habit.

Recognize that worrying is a habit. A habit is something we do, over and over, without even recognizing that we do it. Worrying is such a habit. It's an anxious response that heads us down a path, and once we recognize we've gone too far down that path, we should STOP!

STOP! the habit. Train yourself to recognize when you head down the path of worry. It's as if you come to a fork in the road and choose the worry route. As we worry our way down this path, we can picture a big red and white STOP! sign. That reminds us to pause, take a deep breath, and choose to turn from continuing down that path. Imagine choosing a more positive path instead. A path of praise: instead of worries, we think about what's right and good and hopeful in our lives. Think of thank-you's to God. Or choose a path of promises: instead of worries, we think about one of God's promises. "For nothing is impossible with God" (Luke 1:37). "I am with you always" (Matt. 28:20). "I can do everything through him who gives me strength" (Phil. 4:13).

STOP! the "what if" worries. Sometimes our habit is to let our imaginations run wild with our worries. We start down the path of worry and gain momentum with "what if" worries. We string together a chain of remote or worst-case-scenario possibilities until we have blown a small concern into a major crisis. We have to live in the here and now, not in the world of "what ifs," so picture again that big red and white STOP! sign. And STOP!

Yield! To God. As we STOP! and turn from the path of worry, we see another sign, the big yellow and black Yield! sign, which reminds us to give our worries to God. So take a look at the parts of your worry; pick out the parts that you can do something about, and give the rest to God. Yield to God by turning your worries into a prayer.

Real Mom Story

"Trust Me" by Holly Josey

As our three boys grew and their world began to expand outside the safe walls of our home, I began believing the myth that if their lives are filled with only truth and goodness, then the final result will be young adults that make only wise choices and godly decisions. We were a home-schooling family, so I found it easy to filter and choose only the best of circumstances for the boys. Everything was under my control, and it was an incredibly heavy burden.

In our fifth year of home-schooling, we moved to Houston. Little did we know that our new home was one block away from an exceptional public elementary school. My husband shared with me the leading he felt God giving, a leading to transition from home school to public school. I was devastated at the thought of losing control. I was face to face with the monstrous myth that ruled my life. I didn't want to believe that this change would really happen.

God was graciously, though not comfortably, forcing the myth out of the hidden depths of my heart. What surfaced into the light was the discovery that the myth I lived by was rooted and nurtured in fear. I feared that the endless outpouring of truth and goodness into my sons' lives was about to be taken away from them. Fear is cruel. Fear clouded my hope and choked out my faith. I was broken and at the end of myself.

The new school year was only a short time away. One morning my husband and the boys had gone out for a game of basketball. I sat quietly in the kitchen staring out the window. In my thoughts, I told God that I felt peace to release my children to this decision, but fear of the unknown things to come continued to torment me. God was whispering, "Trust me." This was the moment that changed everything. Yes, God, I *will* trust you. Teach me how. I want you to be in control.

Today our boys are in their second year of public school. My greatest fears have been replaced with quiet, peaceful trust. We allow them their proportioned space and freedom to make choices so that their faith in God can grow. He knows these boys far better than I ever will, and he loves them more than I am humanly capable. I continually hear God whisper, "Trust me." These two words have become my security and peace.

Reality Check

1. Identify some ways you have protected your child in the last week. What has been the benefit of your actions in his or her life?

2. How might your protection of your child need to switch to preparation today? In what areas do you need to step back so that your child can grow?

3. Have you ever identified your main mothering goal for your children? What kind of child do you want to send out the door at age eighteen? What goal will help you know that you've done your best to prepare your child to be this kind of person? Remembering this goal in the midst of mothering will help push you through the temptation to overprotect instead of prepare your children for life.

4. How much do you worry? Are you a constant worrier or a Worry-Some Mom? What can you do to adjust your worry time and move toward trust?

5. Poet Ranier Maria Rilke once wrote, "We need, in love, to practice only this: letting each other go. For holding on comes easily. We do not need to learn it." Does holding on come more easily for you than letting go? How can you adjust your natural inclination to hold on and instead learn to let go?

6. Have you ever really asked God to be responsible for your child? Indeed, do you believe that he loves your child even more than you do? How can you trust him with your child so that as he or she grows, he becomes trustworthy in their lives as well?

For Further Reading

Raising Great Kids by Dr. Henry Cloud and Dr. John Townsend
What Every Child Needs by Elisa Morgan and Carol Kuykendall
Loving and Letting Go by Carol Kuykendall
Tame Your Fears by Carol Kent
Living Fearlessly by Sheila Walsh

Real Moms...

- A real mom encourages her babies to do the next skill, and once her babies roll, crawl, or walk, she silently wishes her babies weren't growing up so fast.

- A real mom tells her husband to take the kids out for a while, and then determines not to worry the whole time they are gone.

- A real mom tries to do what's best for her child.

- A real mom doesn't want to take the training wheels off the bicycle . . . but she does.

Chapter 12

Control Freak Mom

Real Moms Can't Control How Their Kids Turn Out

> I'm going to make a statement that may disturb some who prefer strict, predictable, hard-and-fast formulas for living: There is no absolute guarantee when it comes to rearing a child.
>
> —Chuck Swindoll

Myth: A good mom is responsible for her child's success.

Reality: A real mom can't control how her child turns out.

If we follow the recipe correctly, a muffin mix delivers delightfully dense and flavorful muffins on demand. If we read the road map carefully, navigating directions accurately, we can arrive at any destination, even if we've never visited the city before. If we complete the software tutorial step by step, we can successfully run any program on our computer. Formulas give predictable results for so many of life's tasks. There is a comforting order in this truth. We can count on it. We can control it. We can feel good about it.

But even with the most predictable formulas, there are exceptions and different ways to obtain the desired result. Two plus two equals four. But so does one plus three. And for some things, there seem to be no formulas at all.

With mothering, for instance, there is no formula. No clear linear approach guaranteed to get us to the same successful, predictable place in the end. We don't want to believe this in the beginning. So we learn the hard way.

In the beginning we buy into the myth that A + B = PC (perfect children). So we start working on the A's and B's. If we eat and drink only healthy stuff during pregnancy, our baby will be born healthy. If we steer our children toward a love for green vegetables and away from ice cream, they won't get fat. If we model healthy communication and pray in front of our children at the dinner table, they'll develop a love for family and God. If we speak against the evils of drugs and premarital sex, our kids will avoid those pitfalls.

At first, we swallow whole the myth that as moms we're responsible for how our kids turn out. And we work really hard on our part.

However, at some point between birth and launching, something goes wrong, something unpredictable that we didn't expect, and we begin to wonder, Is this my fault? We face a child with a bent on biting, bed-wetting, a learning disability, a need for braces or glasses or insulin or chemotherapy, and we ask, Did I cause this? We wrestle through bouts of tantrums, lying, cheating, doing drugs, depression, or speeding tickets, and we shudder with the question, Where did this behavior come from? Didn't we do our best? Where did we go wrong?

Slowly we realize there are no guarantees in mothering. But then we might ask ourselves why we ever believed we'd be responsible for the way our kids turned out in the first place. After all, most of us know that while our parents—or lack thereof—may have shaped who we are, those factors did not *make* us who we are today. We played a part in our own growing up process. Yet with our own mothering—handing down life's lessons to our own children—we allow less permission for divergence.

Psychologist Harriet Lerner suggests an explanation in her book *The Mother Dance:* "In a production-oriented society, it's only natural that a mother will want to create a perfect product to prove to herself, her own mother and the world that she's done her job well. We mothers are judged not only by our behavior, but also by our *children's* behavior, which we can influence but not control."[1]

> **Slowly we realize there are no guarantees in mothering.**

We're talking the report-card bit here. This myth that moms are responsible for their kids' success comes from a mom's need to measure her value by them. Kids are a moms' report card. If a kid turns out to be in the National Honor Society, a whiz at athletics, brilliant on stage, advanced in social relationships, *and* hits the missions trip scene with the youth group, well dandy! If not, mom and her investment in that child's life pretty much stinks. Mom's a flop. A flunk in parenting. A failure. "It is the unwritten law of the land that mom will be judged on how well her children behave, perform, succeed in school, and ultimately turn out in life."[2]

Obviously, this myth destroys everything it touches. It leaves both mom and child paralyzed by fear of failure. Impossible expectations yield miserable outcomes.

How insane to try to measure our value and success as moms by how our children turn out, since we have little to no control over their choices! There are no formulas for mothering. No guarantees. In fact, there is not even one recognized standard as to what makes a child a success in adulthood. From the urban young professional to the artsy eccentric, few folks even agree on what's right when it comes to maturity. How can we ever win at this game?

Truth sets us free, mom. Each of our children and each child of every other mom we meet is imprinted with God's unique blueprint for who that child will become. Our job as a mom is to raise up the child—the unique child—God has given us. A familiar Bible verse puts it this way: "Train a child in the way he should go, and when he is old he will not turn from it" (Prov. 22:6). In other words, raise a child *in his way, in the way God made that unique child to be,* and when he is old, he will, indeed, be the person God made him to be. While this passage may underline that our investment "goes into" our child, there is no implication that it will "come out" as we desire—that he will be like us, believe like us, or make choices like us.

There's a key principle here: learning what is possible to control and what is not. Recovering addicts learn the grace of understanding this challenge by living out the words of "The Serenity Prayer," known to help recovering alcoholics in Alcoholics Anonymous. Its truth guides us away from the ridiculous myth that we can actually take responsibility for how another human being turns out in life by controlling their choices. Instead, this prayer slices apart the tangled issues of what we can and can't control, leaving the reality that we are here to influence, to shape, and to guide. "God, grant me the serenity to accept the things I cannot change, the courage to change the things I can, and the wisdom to know the difference."

What we can and can't change has everything to do with what we can and can't control. Serenity comes when we understand the difference. Let's start with what we *can* control as moms. Hmm. Age of successful potty training? Depends. Okay, playmates? Until high school. Dating? Not after they leave home for life on their own, and that's usually when they pick their permanent partners. Mercy.

Real moms know they can control only how they *influence* their children's lives. We know we can set rules and consistently enforce them. We can love our children unconditionally. We can encourage them. We can be their "reminders," helping them discover who God created them to be. We can plant the seeds of faith in their hearts and pray for them unceasingly. In others words, we can control *who we are* in the lives of our children. Besides that, we can control *who we partner with* to raise our child, meaning the father of that child (whether we're married to him or not) and God.

> **Each child has his own free will. God made each of us that way. And each child has her own natural bent or personality or mindset.**

But we can't control *who our child will become*. Each child has his own free will. God made each of us that way. And each child has her own natural bent or personality or mindset.

How silly we are to give in to the myth that we can make our children who we want them to be, or that we are in the end responsible for who they make themselves to be. And what if the result is something we'd never imagined, planned, chosen, or steered toward? What if that result is less than we'd hoped for? Then we sit, head in hands, watching our child choose against and away from all we hold dear, all too quickly concluding we have failed.

Surely Billy and Ruth Graham felt this way when their son, Franklin, bolted from their beliefs and their lifestyle in his late adolescence and young adulthood. Party boy to the max. Were they responsible for the way he was turning out? For his carousing, his rejection of their faith, his rebellion? Were they not the same parents to all his siblings? Take these questions a step further. When

Franklin turned his life around and recommitted to Jesus in his thirties, were his parents then responsible for that step but not the others? Obviously, parents are not responsible for the results either way. But they are responsible for influencing the process in parenting. Billy and Ruth planted the seeds of faith in the hearts of their children at an early age, but Franklin's journey toward personal faith took a different path than his other siblings.

Real moms know what they can control and what they can't control. They clearly know that they are not responsible for the way their kids turn out but rather are responsible to influence their children in the direction of healthy adulthood. They are responsible for loving their children unconditionally, praying unceasingly, and never giving up. But they don't evaluate their worth as mothers based on the choices their children make. They wait and watch and influence, honoring the individual shaping of an individual life by a power beyond themselves, just as they know that same power has shaped their own lives as well. As Abraham Lincoln said, "I have been controlled by some other power than my own will, that I cannot doubt that this power comes from above."[3]

■■■■■ Real Mom Story ■■■■■
"I Wish" by Susan Tuggy

I wish I could keep you from getting hurt . . .
   no cuts,
   no bruises,
   no tears.
I can't.
But I *can* . . .

Are You a Control-Aholic?

Many women load themselves up with unnecessary stress because they need to be in control of their environment, other people, and every situation they find themselves in. Then, when life spins out of their control—as it inevitably will—they're unable to cope. You may be a "control-aholic" if you . . .

- never do anything spontaneous.
- fall apart when your schedule is interrupted.
- have to look just right every time you go out (or even if you're not going out).
- yell at your children excessively about messing up the house. (We've heard of women who vacuum up footprints on the carpet.)
- have to have everything matching.
- spend an inordinate amount of time on planning, organizing, and seeking to emulate that seemingly perfect friend.
- need to know exactly what to expect of a given event or circumstance.
- can't relax until "all the work is done."
- feel uncomfortable with mystery, randomness, unanswered questions. (Many control-aholics need to make sense out of everything, including complex spiritual issues.)[4]

give you a neon orange bandage,
or put some nice cold ice on your owie,
or hug you tight enough to squeeze the tears out.

I wish I could make every day sunny and warm . . .
no storm clouds,
no cold winds,
no smoggy air.
I can't.
But I *can* . . .
give you an umbrella,
or find your warmest jacket,
or do something fun with you inside our home.

I wish I could cook only your most favorite foods every day . . .
no spices,
no squishy squash,
no funny fish.
I can't.
But I *can* . . .
have you try one very small bite,
or put ketchup on it,
or serve it on your favorite plate.

Oh, how I wish I could keep you from getting sick . . .
no runny nose,
no chicken pox,
no tummy ache.
I can't.
But I *can* . . .
help you blow,
or rub lotion on your spots,
or rock you in my arms till you feel better.

I wish I could say everything just right . . .
   no cranky words,
   no hurt feelings,
   no bad days.
   I can't.
But I *can* say . . .
   "I'm sorry,"
   or "Please forgive me,"
   or "Will you ask Jesus to help Mommy?"

Now *that* I can do!

Reality Check

Harriet Lerner, in her book *Mother Dance,* writes, "Consider repeating as a mantra, 'I am responsible for my own behavior; I am not responsible for my child's behavior.' This means you do as good a job as you can and give up the omnipotent fantasy that you can control who your child is or how your child thinks, feels, or behaves."[5]

1. Do you believe the myth that you are responsible for your child's success? Why or why not? How was this myth planted in your thinking? What can you do to untangle this false belief and replace it with truth?

2. What is the difference between controlling and influencing your child? In what ways are you trying to control your child's choices right now? Is what you're pursuing even possible?

3. Assuming you've identified the difference between controlling and influencing your child, how will you move to a position of influencing rather than controlling as your child grows up? How might this changing position free both you and your child? What might such a shift communicate to your child about your confidence in him or her? Explain.

Myths about Mothering

4. Do you tend to evaluate other mothers by how their kids have turned out? Are your conclusions about their investments accurate based on what we've covered in this chapter? Explain.

5. Read Gary Collins' "Truths for Our Families" below. Which statement do you need to consider at a deeper level? Why?

Truths for Our Families

One: Despite all the changes that disrupt families, God is in control.

Two: Even though divorce rates are high, most marriages stay intact.

Three: No family is without problems and periodic crises.

Four: All parents make mistakes, but most kids survive very well.

Five: It is possible to have healthy families even in a chaotic and immoral society.

Six: We can raise kids successfully even if we don't have all the answers.

Seven: The majority of families are not seriously dysfunctional.

Eight: Even good parents sometimes have rebellious kids.

Nine: Even bad parents sometimes have healthy adjusted kids.

Ten: God loves our families.[6]

For Further Reading

Codependent No More by Melodie Beattie
Facing Codependence by Pia Melody
The Mom Factor by Dr. Henry Cloud and Dr. John Townsend
Boundaries by Dr. Henry Cloud and Dr. John Townsend

Real Moms . . .

- A real mom understands that life isn't perfect or doesn't follow certain paths she imagined before her child came along.

- A real mom knows her children won't *always* do what she tells them to do.

- A real mom knows she can't always prevent her children from getting sick, even if she takes good care of them.

3

Myths about More Than Mothering

Chapter 13

Truth is Our Friend Mom

*Real Moms Know the Truth Is Scary
and Can Hurt*

> When we learn that truth is our friend, growth deepens.
>
> —Dr. Henry Cloud and Dr. John Townsend

Myth: A good mom avoids the truth if it is unpleasant.

Reality: A real mom knows the truth is scary and can hurt.

A friend is someone who knows you—and still likes you. A friend is lovingly honest with you. A friend listens and responds, knowingly. A friend challenges you, encourages you, and helps you get to know yourself. A friend wants the best for you. A friend sticks with you through good moments and bad. And somehow, in almost inexplicable ways, a friend helps you grow.

Now, we've all had a friend that we didn't really like in the beginning. She sometimes made us feel a little uncomfortable, and we found ourselves wanting to avoid her. But she was persistent and didn't give up, and over time we realized that she was a faithful friend who was good for us.

Truth is that kind of friend.

We began this book with a challenge to get real. This means dropping the mythical approach to motherhood that aims us toward impossible standards or puts us behind masks. Instead, we are challenged to embrace reality: we're human, fallible, yet talented moms who can make an enormous difference in the lives of our children. When we get real. And so we've tackled myth upon myth—exposing each one of them as lies and suggesting an alternate reality for each.

> **Truth is reality.
> Truth is what is.
> Truth is our friend.**

What we've *really* been talking about in this book is *truth*. Truth *is* reality. Truth is *what is*. While it may not be the kind of friend we initially want in our lives, truth is our friend.

The overall myth of this chapter is this: truth is bad and should be avoided because it can make us uncomfortable. We probably wouldn't pick it out of a crowd and invite it to do lunch. Just the two of us. Face to face with truth. We're kind of afraid of it. We tend to deny its reality.

But guess what? Just like that friend, the truth doesn't go away. So why don't we want truth for our friend? Well, even though truth is our friend, it also can be painful. We don't like pain. For example, admitting that we're Monster Moms at times can be embarrassing and disappointing. Acknowledging that we like some things better than sex makes us fear we're less of a woman. Confessing that we can't do it all, so the answer is no, may jeopardize an important relationship. Myths, or untruths, seem to promise greater comfort and protection.

Truth helps us grow in three practical ways:

1. *Truth moves us toward change.* It makes us look at the need to redirect our thinking, our goals, our pastimes, even some aspects of who we are. Change is uncomfortable and risky. When we recognize that we're not really moms who deal well with boundaries (Please Everyone Moms), and that we need to grow in this area, for our own sake and for the sake of our children, we're cornered with the choice of change. Will we risk *not* doing what we've always done in order to keep things running smoothly in our families? Will we take that risk so that everyone has a better chance to grow?

2. *Truth reveals us to others and deepens our relationships.* If we're going to stand for what we really think, then others will know who we really are, and they may not like what they see or hear. We may not get the instant affirmation or gratification we like. We might be ridiculed, criticized, even rejected. Who wants that? Isn't it just easier to be what others might *expect* us to be in many moments, to hide behind a mask instead of reveal the Real Me Mom for who she is?

Author and mother Ruth Haley Barton says, "Yes, truth-telling can be frightening. But the alternative is much worse. When we cannot bring ourselves to tell the truth in our relationships, they will stay at a surface level at best; it is even more likely that they will deteriorate and die. Misunderstandings arise but are never resolved. Feelings beg to be shared but are left to fester inside. Offenses occur but nobody talks about them. Our true personalities are hidden and never invited to flourish in the warmth of acceptance. Avoidance patterns set in. Hurt and misunderstanding lead to detachment, distrust, and bitterness. And love begins to die."[1]

What *is* can be tough. Reality bites. Truth hurts.

3. *But truth also frees us.* Truth is friend enough to *use* the pain to help us grow to a better place. When Jesus tells his disciples, "Then you will know the truth, and the truth will set you free" (John 8:32), he is referring to how God's grace can free us from sin. The image he uses is one of slavery. (You know, being "owned," so to speak.) When we get our minds wrapped around the whole concept that God loves us enough to allow his son, Jesus, to die on a cross as payment for *our* wrongs, and accept that as truth—wow— then we're *freed* from the contortions and burdens of mythical thinking. We're freed to be different, to be better.

Knowing the truth grows us into the freedom to live out that truth in our days.

- We overcome a fear that we won't be accepted and then we are *free* to know who we are and to be who we are as the Real Me Moms God created us to be.
- We wrestle daily with guilt as Perma-Guilt Moms, but we also become *free* to move past its manipulation and power over our every minute.
- We expose our human emotion of anger and obtain *freedom* to process how we handle that anger as Monster Moms.
- We release ourselves from the pressure and responsibility to make life happy-dappy for everyone else around us and receive the *freedom* to move beyond being Please Everyone Moms.
- We *free* ourselves to accept our bodies and make the most of our appearance, knowing that we are Lookin' Good Enough Moms.
- We have the *freedom* to acknowledge our feelings about sex and push on toward better sex with our husbands by enjoying life as Viagra Moms.

- We let go of the impossible expectations of perfectionism and discover the *freedom* to become Doin' My Best Moms.
- We lay aside our way as the only way and find *freedom* as Mommy Wars Moms who accept others even though they mother differently than we do.
- We readily admit that we can't do motherhood on our own and *freely* welcome help from others as S.O.S. Moms.
- We acknowledge the reality of busyness but also recognize we have the *freedom* to choose what we'll be busy with as Busy Moms.
- We become Worry-Some Moms by *freeing* ourselves to allow the painful stuff in life to prepare our kids for their futures.

> **Truth is the best friend a mom can have.**

- We *free* ourselves with the reality that we are not responsible for how our kids turn out as Control Freak Moms.

Truth is our friend. It helps us grow. We are challenged by the truth. We are changed by the truth. The truth sets us free. It makes us better. Knowing the truth frees us to live the truth out in our lives. Real moms learn to pick our friend—the truth—out of the crowd of myths every time, convinced that truth is the best friend a mom can have.

■■■ Real Mom Story ■■■
"True Feelings" by Rebecca Pippert

I know a woman who is a very angry, difficult person. Once, she really let me have it, in a nonstop, high-decibel diatribe. I listened carefully, and where I could honestly acknowledge what I thought was my fault, I did. Later I told her that although I loved

Truths That Set Us Free

- God loves you.
- God forgives you.
- God is growing you into who he created you to be.
- God is with you—always.
- God is good.
- God never changes. He's the same every single day.
- God cares about what you care about.
- God loves your kids even more than you do.
- God doesn't make mistakes. He's perfect.
- God loves you too much to leave you the way you are.
- God meets all of your needs.
- God loves you no matter what you've done, no matter what you will do. You can't change his love for you.
- God can be trusted.
- God wants you to have his best.
- God is enough.
- God keeps all of his promises.

her, I was deeply troubled by her style and some of the harsh content of her attack. When I recounted to a friend what I'd said to her, he surprised me by saying, "Yes, Becky, I know you want to love her."

That was all it took to break through my denial. I saw in a flash that although I wanted to love her, the truth was I didn't even like her. In fact, I couldn't stand her. There are other difficult people in my life I do love, but not this one. Why did I say just the opposite? Was I being intentionally dishonest? No, I didn't recognize my true feelings even though they were right under the surface. I was denying them because to acknowledge to myself such an intense dislike for someone threatened my view of myself as the loving person I longed to be.

But to be honest about the way I really felt brought a great sense of relief. Jesus wasn't kidding when he said the truth shall set you free. It wasn't that I abandoned my determination to love her, or that I went to her in my new freedom and said in a blaze of glory, "I finally figured it out: I can't stand you! You make me sick!" It was that now I knew where I needed God's help. How could I ask for help for a problem I hadn't acknowledged?[2]

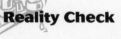

Reality Check

1. Do you view truth as your friend? In what ways? How does relating to truth as your friend help you grow?

2. What myths listed in this chapter have the greatest hold on you? What truths can replace these myths and help you grow toward freedom?

3. Have you been hurt by the truth? Think of an example. How did that pain grow you and make you better?

4. Author Ken Gire suggests, "The 'oughts' will keep us from telling the truth."[3] What does this statement mean?

5. What steps could you take to welcome truth into your life as your friend?

6. What are some truths you readily accept?

For Further Reading

How People Grow by Dr. Henry Cloud and Dr. John Townsend
Hope Has Its Reasons by Rebecca Manley Pippert
Telling Yourself the Truth by Marie Chapian
The Truth That Frees Us by Ruth Haley Barton

Real Moms . . .

- A real mom still loves her kids even when they tell her, " I drew a picture of you and then I scratched you out!"

- A real mom gets up her nerve to talk through a conflict when she'd rather believe it will just go away.

- A real mom asks a friend to tell her the truth.

Myths about More Than Mothering

Chapter 14

Soul Mom

Real Moms Are More Than Moms

> The soul hardly ever realizes it, but whether (she) is a believer or not, (her) loneliness is really a homesickness for God.
>
> —Hubert Van Zeller

Myth: A good mom finds her sole purpose in raising children.

Reality: A real mom is more than a mom.

When we're moms, we often think that life is all about our kids and our being a good mom to them. What we invest in them. The choices we make to be there or not be there for them, day in and day out. How they turn out. Goodness, this focus starts during pregnancy when the whole goal is to keep them healthy in utero and then to get them out safely. Once they're born, we aim for the next milestone: sleeping through the night. Then it's sitting up, eating right, growing well, crawling, walking, talking, crossing the street, spending the night out, school, driving, dating, graduating, marrying, having kids who become our grandkids, and then poof—we're done. We die. When we reach the end of our lives and look back over the journey, we see that it's all about being a good mom to our kids.

> **God made moms to be more than moms.**

Or is it? Maybe we've just uncovered yet another myth to shatter: that the purpose of life for moms is pretty much about our kids. That's it. If we do get them raised, then we're doing what really matters, what we were made for.

Except we're made for more. Sure, moms are moms forever and mothering matters incredibly. In fact, when we get to the end and look back, not much matters more in life than the investment we make in our children. Not much. But there is *something*.

See, God made moms to be more than moms. Does that sound surprising? He made us eternal beings, created by and connected to him for a relationship with him and his world—for eternal purposes—that includes being moms, and more. We can be truly free only when we know this and live it too. That's a mouthful and a brainful, but it's the truth.

There it is again: the truth.

God wants to find us. He wants to be in a relationship with us in which he can give what he wants us to have. He offers freedom when we receive what he holds out to us: truth.

"I stand at the door and knock," God tells us in the Bible. "If anyone hears my voice and opens the door, I will come in and eat with him, and he with me" (Rev. 3:20 NIV). God desires our relationship and stands ready with his presence. We simply need to respond and to receive his truth and love.

Henri Nouwen describes it this way: "The question is not 'How am I to find God?' but 'How am I to let myself be found by him?' The question is not 'How am I to know God?' but 'How am

I to let myself be known by God?' And finally, the question is not 'How am I to love God?' but 'How am I to let myself be loved by God?' God is looking into the distance for me, trying to find me, and longing to bring me home."[1]

The truth that God loves us so much that his son died on a cross to pay the penalty for our sins sets us free when we know that truth and when we live it out by receiving God and all he wants to give us. We're moms. But we're more than moms. We're connected to the living God in a relationship that puts us on a lifelong journey into eternity and gives us kingdom purposes in life here on earth now. Wow! No wonder that when we understand this truth, we fulfill the potential we uniquely possess for God and his world.

Do you know what "kingdom purposes" are? Kingdom purposes are investments we make with our lives that last beyond today and reach into eternity. Of course they include our investment in our children and other family members. But kingdom purposes also include investments in others—friends, neighbors, coworkers—and in projects that will last and make a difference for God in our world.

Pastor and writer Gordon MacDonald observes, "A crucial part of real-world faith building . . . is to connect one's life to an overarching dream or a consuming idea. . . . For centuries, people have speculated about the key change that Jesus instigated in the lives of His followers when He came to this world. I believe the key change was the dream He gave them—the dream of the kingdom of God."[2]

Further, when we don't know our kingdom purpose, we experience a kind of frustration. But when we do know what we're about with our lives, we discover a unique contentment in our days.

Soul Moms know they are more than moms. They can see above and beyond the struggle of getting their child on schedule with potty training to focus on the greater purposes of raising that child. They can be content with doing their best as moms, which is not perfect, because they can put their daily challenges into a greater eternal perspective. They know that there's more to life than mothering because they are more than moms and because they are involved in other kingdom-building pursuits in the midst of their mothering. They know that living this truth out helps them and helps their children, as this mother observes:

> I have adjusted and reworked my commitments to my own spiritual development, family, and vocation in several different ways, learning more and more how to be responsive to the truest needs and invitations of that particular time and season. Although as a family we still sometimes wrestle with scheduling and priorities, we have worked more consciously toward a configuration in our family life that supports the [Kingdom] calling of each one of us. . . . It has been good for our daughters to understand and observe their mother as a woman who not only is committed to them but, at the same time, is also called to contribute in the larger community of faith and the world. I am glad that they have seen several models of what's possible for them as women, should they also be called to combine motherhood with other life callings.[3]

Soul Moms are real moms who take a deep breath and raise their gaze. They mother day by day, reaching toward their child's launching, *because* they are more than moms. They know the investments they make in the lives of their children stretch beyond their children to the people their children will touch, and their children, and their children.

"I've Got to Talk to Somebody, God" by Marjorie Holmes

There are all these walls between us—husband and wife, parent and child, neighbor and neighbor, friend and friend.

Walls of self. Walls of silence. Even walls of words.

For even when we try to talk to each other, new walls begin to rise. We camouflage, we hold back, we make ourselves sound better than we really are. Or we are shocked and hurt by what is revealed. Or we sit privately in judgment, criticizing even when we pretend to agree.

But with you, Lord, there are no walls.

You, who made me, know my deepest emotions, my most secret thoughts. You know the good of me and the bad of me; you already understand.

Why, then, do I turn to you?

Because as I talk to you, my disappointments are eased, my joys are enhanced. I find solutions to my problems or the strength to endure what I must.

From your perfect understanding, I receive understanding for my own life's needs.

Thank you that I can always turn to you; I've got to talk to somebody, God.[4]

Letting God Find You

God reveals himself most clearly to us through his son, Jesus, his Word, the Bible, and through the gathering of his people, the church. These are foundational aspects of how we, as Christians, know God. But because God is a personal God, each of us senses his loving presence in other ways as well. These expressions can never substitute for the fundamental ways we know God. They can only enhance our personal relationship with him. Gary Thomas suggests the following various "sacred pathways" for drawing near to God. Which one describes you?

Meeting God out of doors (Naturalists). Naturalists find God outdoors. They experience a sense of worship by a river more than in a building and learn something about God by watching an ant farm.

Meeting God with the senses (Sensates). Sensates use their senses to experience God. They seek to be overwhelmed by sights, sounds, and smells. They experience God in liturgy, in art, in music, and in architecture.

Meeting God through ritual and symbol (Traditionalists). Traditionalists tend to lead structured and disciplined lives, following traditions of the Christian faith such as attending church and tithing. They meet God in historical practices and might find unstructured, solitary worship difficult.

Meeting God in solitude and simplicity (Ascetics). Ascetics long for solitude, a place alone with no noise or distractions where they can pray. They are drawn to introspections and simplicity, blossoming in a world of solitude, strictness, and austerity.

Meeting God through confrontation (Activists). Activists meet God on the battlefield, where they fight against evil and share their beliefs. They are extroverts and find actions and confrontation to be spiritually filling.

Meeting God by loving others (Caregivers). Caregivers build a faith and a relationship with God through serving others. Their compassion and open hearts often bring them to the poor and needy, where they experience a fuller knowledge of God.

Meeting God through mystery and celebration (Enthusiasts). Enthusiasts are inspired by mystery and celebration. Emotional people, they want to be excited, to dance and sing. Enthusiasts experience God best when they are moved by their experiences.

Meeting God through adoration (Contemplatives). Contemplatives seek a deep love relationship with God. A contemplative will be most content if she feels she is sitting at the feet of God, deepening her love relationship with him.

Meeting God with the mind (Intellectuals). Intellectuals live in the world of concepts. They meet God through study of his Word, history, theology, and other religions. They want to understand more than feel.[5]

Reality Check

1. Have you ever begun a relationship with God by receiving his love for you? Praying a simple prayer is all it takes. "Dear Jesus, I want to let you find me, know me, love me, bring me 'home' into a relationship with you. I know I am not perfect—far from it—and that I need your forgiveness for my sins, my mistakes, and my shortcomings. Please forgive me. I want to trust you as my Savior and I want to know you as my Lord. Please come into my life and begin a relationship with me. Amen."

2. Surrender is an important practice for moms. We often begin to understand it in our relationships with God. Can you surrender your guilt, your fears, your self, and your children to God's care?

3. What does this sentence mean to you: "Moms are more than moms"?

4. When you raise your gaze and look into and beyond mothering with an eternal perspective, what kind of kingdom dreams do you think God might have for you? How do those fit with the dreams you have for yourself? What kingdom dreams do you have for your children?

5. Look beyond your active years of mothering to other seasons in your life. How might God be growing you today for his purposes for your life in the future?

For Further Reading

The Contemplative Mom by Ann Kroeker
Sacred Pathways by Gary Thomas
Seeking the Face of God by Gary Thomas
Soul Keeping by Howard Baker
The Reflective Life by Ken Gire
When the Soul Listens by Jan Johnson
The Return of the Prodigal Son by Henri Nouwen
The Ragamuffin Gospel by Brennan Manning
Becoming a Woman of Influence by Carol Kent
Mom's Devotional Bible

Real Moms . . .

- A real mom knows she needs God.
- A real mom struggles to stay connected to God just when she needs him the most.
- A real mom falls asleep praying for her kids.
- A real mom knows that mothering matters . . . and so do other things.
- A real mom knows she is loved by a real God.

Chapter 15

Forever Mom

*Real Moms Know Mothering
Gets Different, Not Easier*

> Someday, somewhere, I shall see what my life has
> come to mean to those who have watched me live.
> —Virgil Reed

Myth: A good mother thinks mothering will get easier.

Reality: A real mom knows mothering doesn't get
easier. It just gets different.

I can't wait until she sleeps through the night. I can't wait until he's walking. I can't wait until she's out of diapers. I can't wait until he's in school. We declare our anticipations in a myriad of ages and stages. We can't wait . . . until we get to the easier part of mothering! Won't life be grand then?

Lodged beneath this impatience is the myth that one day, mothering will get easier. That at some point, we will round the corner and labor past the really hard stuff. Then it's simply a downhill joyride from there.

Guess what? Mothering doesn't really get easier. It just gets different. In the infant years, we struggle to find enough physical energy to face yet another day of teething. In toddlerhood, we chase our escape-artist explorers and perform calisthenics to create barriers between them and danger. Then when they finally go off to preschool, we deal with social issues, like why do they bite other kids and refuse to share? Next come the elementary years. Whew! But here come parent-teacher conferences, after-school activities, and coping with the ups and downs of fickle friendships. On to middle school with the assault

> **Mothering just changes. And the challenges—though different—never end.**

of values on thinking, pleas for items to fulfill the latest trends, and, joy of joys, puberty. More new worries. Oh, and then there's high school and the confusion of independence issues with slammed doors, moody silences, hogged phones and computers, and rolled-eyed responses. From there it's post-high-school choices, marriage partners, and job successes.

On and on the challenges go. When we get to the destination we eagerly anticipated, we discover "destination disappointment" and new frustrations. Ask any mother of a teenager, a college kid, a young adult, a middle-aged adult. Easier? Not exactly. Mothering just changes. And the challenges—though different—never end.

So why do we get ourselves tangled up in the myth that mothering will get easier? Why do we set ourselves up for disappointment at these destinations? Is it our naive optimism, fueled by living in a task-oriented society? Or have we simply not accumulated enough life experiences to know the truth? In mothering, as in most of life, things don't get easier. They just get different. There is no great finish line marking the end, because the only finish line is death. You know, *really* being done. We are Forever Moms, on a forever journey to influence our children and to be influenced by them—until death do we part.

So how do we make a go of our role as Forever Moms?

We see the journey as an ongoing adventure of discovery in which every day and every year and every milestone gives us greater freedom to mellow out and enjoy the moment we're living. Unfortunately, that perspective usually comes from older people looking back on life. "Life would be infinitely happier if we could only be born at the age of 80 and gradually approach 18," Mark Twain said. If we could live life backward, applying what we learn along the way, we'd lighten up more and sweat the small stuff less. Instead of trying to grin and bear it, we'd grin and savor it. The passing years give us an understanding for how the truth really does set us free.

This accumulated wisdom often prompts older people to wonder how they would live life over. One woman wrote, "I'd dare to make more mistakes. . . . I would be sillier. . . . I would take fewer things seriously. I would take more chances. . . . I would eat more ice cream and less beans. . . . I would start barefoot earlier in the spring and stay that way later in the fall. I would go to more dances. I would ride more merry-go-rounds. I would pick more daisies."[1]

Our mothering journey is only a part of an exciting larger life journey in which we keep learning to live out the truth we receive in our relationship with God and with others. It's the kind of truth that makes us more real and sets us free to enjoy mothering.

We are moms forever who are forever applying this wisdom in the midst of mothering:

- We learn to live in the present age and stage without longing for the next. Granted, we all wince when the grandma in the grocery store pinches our toddler's cheek and tells us these are the best days of our lives, just as we find gum in our hair and that "precious" toddler begins to throw a tantrum because we won't buy him what he wants. Yet there is a shred of truth in her words. We will never return to this age and stage again. Memorize the moments. Make the most of life's irretrievable moments. Live today and worry about tomorrow later. This is a milestone day on your mothering timeline which will never come around again. Don't miss it.

- We look for the "aha!" moments. We all stumble upon little discoveries, when we learn something we hadn't known. These become stepping stones on our forever journey. Prior to having children, did you ever understand the meaning of sacrificial love, which helps you understand God's love for us? Before you had a child with a learning disability, what did you really know about the reading process? Notice what you're learning through motherhood and how these "aha!" moments help you understand the meaning of the overall journey of your life.

- We expect the hard stuff at all the ages and stages. Each developmental season has both its joys and challenges. We're better prepared when we see them as normal and ready ourselves to face them. Join a support group of moms, where you can swap ideas. Find a mentor who's a few steps ahead of you on the journey and ask her questions. Get over the illusion that life will be cake at some point and face reality.

- We get growing! No, we can't pole-vault over the hard stuff today, but we can make a plan for how we will grow bit by bit between today and tomorrow. Do you have a dream about how you'd like to develop your nonmothering talents? Take an afternoon sabbatical alone somewhere and write out your plan with one goal per year that will move you closer to your dream. Okay, so you can't start renovating old houses while mothering three preschoolers.

But can you save a little money every month toward this dream? Or take a class on remodeling? Set aside some ideas for the tomorrows that will, indeed, come.

- We keep on loving our children. Through the seasons, we will constantly change the way we show our love for them. But the foreverness of their need for love in each stage mirrors our own. Paul writes to the Corinthians in one of the most famous verses in the Bible that "Love never fails. . . . Now these three remain: faith, hope and love. But the greatest of these is love" (1 Cor. 13:8; 13). Real moms know that our children need our love forever, though its shape will change as our children change.

Real moms know that mothering doesn't get easier and welcome the reality that it will get different. The joy is discovering that as we change and shape our children, they also change and shape us, and the generations keep coming, and the legacies get passed on. We experience the seamless circle of God's love, passed on and on and on. Daughters become mothers . . . and mothers become grandmothers and we finally "get it" as we understand that mothering never ends.

Season to season, mothering stretches us, deepens us, and makes us more real. Real moms live out this truth in life . . . forever.

═══ Real Mom Story ═══

"Mother Never Told Me" by Heather Harpham

The other day I stood forever in the wrapping-paper section of the grocery store trying to select a Mother's Day card. I would pick one up, read the first two lines, choke on the sap, and replace it. Don't the people who write these cards *realize* that most of us grew up in the same house with our mothers?

Self-Discovery

The journey of mothering is an incredible journey of self dis-covery. What have you learned about yourself since you became a mother? What do you think about most? How do you spend your time and money? Who do you admire and what do you laugh at? These are simple questions, but to have more fun on the journey of self discovery, try answering these questions, which are typical college-application essay questions, aimed at getting to know the potential freshman:

- What do the contents of your closet reflect about you?

- Describe your earliest memory and how it reflects the person you are today.

- With which literary character do you most readily identify and why?

- Imagine you attend your twentieth high-school reunion. Among your former classmates are sev-eral millionaires, a best-selling novelist, and the President of the United States. But your classmates have chosen you as the guest of honor. Why?

- If you were given 10 million dollars but could not spend any of it on yourself, how would you spend it?

- What is written on page 227 of your autobiography?

I had a good mom. But she didn't dry every tear I shed, shine like a beacon in my darkest hours, and spend her every waking moment trying to add that "special touch" to our family.

Far from being pink, flowered, and pressed neatly into a card, Mom wore an aged pea-green bathrobe and often spoke anything but poetic lines. I remember when she was haggard and crabby and when she ran through the house slamming doors and crying that "nobody cares!"

I recall these things now more than ever. Perhaps that's because I've joined her in the Mother World where children don't care if Dobson said it would work and where toddlers delight in demolishing tidy rooms just before company comes. I too have screamed on occasion, "Nobody cares!" And sometimes I've even believed it for a little while.

Of course, I didn't know it would be like this. No mother ever really does, or children might become an endangered species. I started out like most moms do—in pursuit of an ideal. I read up on parenting, studied the Bible, and aspired to become like the woman in Proverbs 31.

I was careful to teach my children about God, his goodness, his love for all creatures. And then, just when I thought my kids might be turning out to be sensitive, loving little boys, I found them on the back patio with a magnifying glass frying ants to death in the hot sun.

I tried to love my children unconditionally, imagining my devotion for them would never wane. But then the feelings sometimes did—especially when their hair got too long and scraggly. After they got it cut and came home all cute and clean-looking, I'd feel guilty about how much more I liked them.

One day as I was busily picking something unrecognizable out of my carpet, I found myself resenting the fact that she, the Proverbs 31 woman, never had children who chewed bubble gum. Her kids probably didn't scribble on her furniture with magic markers either, I thought with a huff, so it's no wonder she could laugh at the days to come.

I began to doubt that my children would ever rise up and call me blessed, although they often rise up and call me mean. The truth sank in that I was failing. And I realized that someday my own kids would grow old standing in a Hallmark shop trying to pick out a Mother's Day card for me. I was contemplating such future glory one afternoon recently when I thought I heard God chime in with a TV commercial, "It doesn't get any better than this."

"What on earth do you mean?" I asked, gazing around me at the commotion, messes, and what I assumed to be catsup on the kitchen wall. Gradually it dawned on me. God was trying to tell me I was normal, an okay mom, the "real thing."

"But what about the gap?" I protested. "What about the gap between me and the Proverbs 31 woman?"

Then I saw that it was him, laying down his life, connecting the "real" and the "ideal" forever. I recalled how God delights in processes, how he laughs with me, and I began to have hope.

That must be why I finally picked out a card for my mom that flowered and frilled, mushed and gushed, and basically called her "blessed." After all, she was a real mom in pursuit of an ideal, too. And now I know how close she really came.[2]

Reality Check

1. In what ways have you been telling yourself that mothering will get easier? What sources feed this myth in your life? What are some of the "destination disappointments" you've experienced?

2. How do you change the shape of your love for your children as they age?

3. What are some "aha!" moments of your mothering? What do you hope your children will remember most about you when they grow up?

4. If you were to write how you would live your life over, what thoughts would you include?

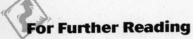

For Further Reading

She Can Laugh At the Days to Come by Valerie Bell
Passages by Gail Sheehy
Emotional Phases of a Woman's Life by Jean Lush
A Mother's Footprints of Faith by Carol Kuykendall

Real Moms . . .

- A real mom knows that childhood passes so quickly—but not quick enough some days.

- A real mom cries when her toddlers cling to her, when her teenagers reject her, and when her own mom is aging.

- A real mom gets tired, frustrated, and loses her patience often; but deep down inside, she knows she'll miss even these times as they grow.

Get Real!

Dear Mom,

We began this book with a "once upon a time" story of a young woman facing the reality of being a mom in the middle of the many myths of mothering. Her unanswered question was, "How do I live happily ever after?"

Let's get real. There is no simple answer to that question. In the last fifteen chapters, we've dealt with the most common myths of mothering and the tensions we all face in trying to live somewhere in between fairy tale expectations and real-life realities. We all long to live more fully and authentically—and therefore to become more like the people God created us to be.

Obviously, this is not an easy process. Choosing to be a real mom in a world filled with unrealistic expectations is tough. Being real often feels risky. It takes hard work. We won't always do it right. We'll experience plenty of guilt along the way. And the journey to becoming real is a slow-paced process of changes and choices that continue for a lifetime.

While we're being real here, as the authors of this book, we'd like to confess that we've learned lots about ourselves while researching and writing about real moms. The questions we've posed in this book are our questions too. Where do these mothering myths come from? Why do we believe them? What's the way out of their tangly hold on us?

Through the years, we've hidden behind our own mythical good-mommy masks. Standing in the preschool parking lot, we smile and talk to another mother about our good children, who aren't being a bit good at that moment. Behind the smiling mask is the distinct desire to stuff our children into *her* minivan that day and zoom away, all alone to some quiet sunny resort in St. Thomas.

Don't get us wrong. Mothering is mostly filled with fabulous moments when our love for our children is beyond description. But we also acknowledge the hard parts that confuse and stretch us. The goal of becoming real, in the midst of this everyday honest life, is not intended to give us just one more impossible goal to reach as moms. The goal is to open our eyes to the kind of freedom we can experience—as women and as moms—in relationship with others, while discovering who we are and growing toward who we are becoming.

The reality is that a mother's journey to being real is filled with tough, life-stretching choices, but the most eternal, greatest truth is that we do not walk that journey alone. We walk alongside a Savior who keeps pointing out the way and keeps giving us his promises, the truths that we can stand on as we face our challenges. The truths that set us free to keep going—and growing.

Forget "happily ever after." Get real. And become the best mom you can be.

Because mothering matters,

Elisa Morgan and Carol Kuykendall

Notes

Chapter 1: Real Me Mom

1. Anna Quindlen, "Playing God on No Sleep," *Newsweek* (2 July, 2001): 64.

2. Charles Swindoll, *Wisdom for the Way* (Nashville: J. Countryman, 2001), 216. (Originally printed in Charles Swindoll, *Growing Wise in Family Life*.)

3. Ken Gire, *The Weathering Grace of God* (Ann Arbor: Servant, 2001), 101.

Chapter 2: Perma-Guilt Mom

1. Harriet Lerner, *The Mother Dance* (New York: HarperPerennial, 1998), 75.

2. Adapted from Dr. Henry Cloud and Dr. John Townsend, *Twelve Christian Beliefs That Can Drive You Crazy* (Grand Rapids, Mich.: Zondervan, 1994), 15.

3. Stormie Omartian, *The Power of a Praying Husband* (Eugene, Ore.: Harvest House, 2001), 67.

Chapter 3: Monster Mom

1. Lisa Moffitt, "Momzilla Finds an 'Attitude Adjuster,'" *Ashland City Times*.

Chapter 4: Please Everyone Mom

1. Anne Morrow Lindbergh, *Gift from the Sea* (New York: Pantheon, 1975), 39.

2. Dr. Henry Cloud and Dr. John Townsend, *Boundaries* (Grand Rapids, Mich.: Zondervan, 1992), 29.

3. John Rosemond, "Hey, Mom! Get a Life!" *Better Homes and Gardens* (May 1996): 106.

4. Dr. Henry Cloud and Dr. John Townsend, *The Mom Factor* (Grand Rapids, Mich.: Zondervan, 1996), 58.

5. Ibid., 60.

6. Cloud and Townsend, *Boundaries*, 50–51.

7. Susan Lawless, "A Little Space Is Every Mom's Simple Wish," *Ashland City Times*.

Chapter 5: Lookin' Good Enough Mom

1. Karen Lee Fontaine, "The Conspiracy of Culture: Women's Issues in Body Size," *Nursing Clinics of North America* 26, no. 3 (September 1991): 673.

2. Vicki Iovine, *The Girlfriends' Guide to Pregnancy* (New York: Pocket Books, 1995), 247–50.

3. Marcia Germaine Hutchinson, *Love the Body You Have* (Freedom, Calif.: Crossing Press, 1985), 16.

Chapter 6: Viagra Mom

1. Dr. Ruth Westheimer, "Love of Chocolate Doesn't Equal Lack of Sex," *Boulder Daily Camera* (4 February, 2002): 8C.

2. Linda Dillow and Lorraine Pintus, *Intimate Issues* (Colorado Springs, Colo.: WaterBrook, 1999), 67.

3. Archibald D. Hart, Ph.D., Catherine Hart Weber, Ph.D., Debra Taylor, M.A., *Secrets of Eve* (Nashville: Word, 1998), 114–15.

4. Dr. Elena Kamel, OB/GYN, Northwestern Memorial Hospital, Chicago, quoted on Oprah's website: www.oprah.com/health/sexuality/health_sex_dys_c.jhtml.

5. David Arp and Claudia Arp, *Love Life for Parents* (Grand Rapids, Mich.: Zondervan, 1998), 97.

6. Joyce Maynard, "Life without Father," *Mc Call's* (August 1984): 78.

7. Dr. Jennifer Berman and Dr. Laura Berman, quoted on Oprah's website: www.oprah.com/tows/pastshows/tows_past_20010207_b.jhtml.

8. Steve Tracy, "The Marriage Mystery," *Christianity Today* (7 January 2002): 63.

9. Hart, Weber, Tayor, *Secrets of Eve*, 41–56.

10. Lisa Moffitt, "Romantic Parents? The Ultimate Oxymoron," *Ashland City Times*.

Chapter 7: Doin' My Best Mom

1. Dr. Henry Cloud and Dr. JohnTownsend, *The Mom Factor* (Grand Rapids, Mich.: Zondervan, 1996), 226.

2. Ibid., 227.

Chapter 8: Mommy Wars Mom

1. Anna Quindlen, "Confessions of a Modern Mom," *Reader's Digest* (August 1988): 85–86.

2. Brenda Quinn, "To Judge or Not to Judge," *ParentLife* (November 2001): 20–21.